Terrific Women Teachers

The Women's Hall of Fame Series

Terrific Women Teachers

Helen Wolfe

Second Story Press

Library and Archives Canada Cataloguing in Publication

Wolfe, Helen, 1953-
Terrific women teachers / by Helen Wolfe.

(The women's hall of fame series)
Includes bibliographical references.
ISBN 978-1-897187-86-9

1. Women teachers—Biography—Juvenile literature.
I. Title. II. Series: Women's hall of fame series

LA2303.W65 2011   j371.10092'2   C2011-900077-6

Editor: Sheba Meland
Designer: Melissa Kaita
Cover photos and icons © istockphoto.com

Printed and bound in Canada

*Second Story Press gratefully acknowledges the support of the Ontario Arts
Council and the Canada Council for the Arts for our publishing program.
We acknowledge the financial support of the Government of Canada through the
Book Publishing Industry Development Program.*

ONTARIO ARTS COUNCIL
CONSEIL DES ARTS DE L'ONTARIO

Canada Council   Conseil des Arts
for the Arts   du Canada

FSC
www.fsc.org

MIX
Paper from
responsible sources
FSC® C004071

Published by
Second Story Press
20 Maud Street, Suite 401
Toronto, ON
M5V 2M5
www.secondstorypress.ca

This book is dedicated to my mother, Toby Wolfe. Although she passed away many years ago, her love and support is and will always be a constant source of strength to me. With her unconditional love, my mother encouraged me to achieve my goals and was the first one to congratulate me whenever I did. She was never a teacher herself, but every day through her example she taught me whatever I understand about personal courage, determination, and conquering obstacles that come our way.

Contents

Introduction

Think about it for a minute. Teachers are a huge part of our lives.

Many kids meet their first teachers at daycare, before they can even walk or talk. Those first teachers are very important. Not only do they care for and nurture very young children while their parents go to work, but they also introduce them to the alphabet, language, and numbers, using games and music. Once we are in school, our teachers help us to read, write, do math and science, and sometimes even lend us a hand in solving our day-to-day problems.

If we're lucky, we've met teachers who have made a big difference in our lives. Sometimes it may be for the ideas they have shared with us, ideas that struck a chord deep inside, and that will remain with us forever. But, more often than not, we love and remember teachers not because of what they taught us, but because of who they are. The most memorable teachers are our role models, those who guide us toward being better people by their own examples.

Not surprisingly, teachers become attached to their students as well. I've been a teacher for more than thirty years, and have had the chance to spend time with many different kinds of students—from kids with special needs to adults who are learning English as a second language. I feel fortunate to have taught some unforgettable students in my classes, and I have such warm memories of those experiences. I really believe that I've learned much more from my students than they may have learned from me.

Some of the teachers you will meet here lived long ago, and paved the way for how I teach my students today, while others are admirable teachers of my own time. Several of the teachers in this book had major obstacles to overcome when they were young girls. Annie Sullivan Macy grew up almost blind, and lost all of her family when she was just a child. She spent most of her childhood in an institution. But with intelligence, hard work and determination, she became a celebrated teacher whose lifelong dedication opened up the world to her student. In turn, Annie's student, Helen Keller, who was mute, deaf, and blind, grew up to be a world-famous educator and advocate for deaf and blind people. Another specially challenged teacher, Denise Fruchter, was a young girl with brain disabilities who struggled at school, and could not enjoy the summer camp experiences that most of us take for granted. There were no camp counselors who understood what she was going through or could help her. So, when she grew up, she created a camp where kids with brain disabilities could have fun and learn many new things, just like everyone else.

Teachers in big cities have their own challenges to overcome. Marva Collins taught as a substitute teacher for many years in poor, inner-city schools, and realized that her students were not being encouraged to excel in high school and go on to college or university. A strongly opinionated woman, Marva decided to open a school that set extremely high expectations of both teachers and students. Very simply, she would not allow students to fail or do less than they were capable of.

Erin Gruwell was a student teacher working with a multicultural group of students who could not get along with each other. In fact, they couldn't sit in the same classroom and have simple discussions without calling each other names and getting into fights. So, Erin created the Freedom Writers project where her students from violent and crime-filled neighborhoods could share their feelings online, and learn more about each other. Hundreds of years earlier, and against everyone's advice, pioneer teacher Onésime Dorval also blazed new trails in bringing students together. She left her comfortable home in Quebec to teach Aboriginal people in isolated communities, earning their love and trust with her devotion and respect for their language and traditions.

These exceptional women teachers are part of this book because they knew that their students should not be defeated because of their environments. These teachers were determined that the kids they taught would be successful, no matter what odds were stacked against them.

You'll also read about several pathfinders who didn't plan to be teachers, but made amazing contributions to education nonetheless. Maria Montessori started out as a doctor—the first woman doctor in Italy. One of Maria's early jobs was as supervisor of a primary school. She could see that lots of kids just couldn't learn much in that strict environment. Maria became the first educator to create a classroom where children could sit in different groups throughout the day, learning skills and exploring their creativity. The kind of classroom that Maria created so many years ago is still with us today.

Raden Ayu Kartini lived in Indonesia all of her life. More than 150 years ago, when education was not available to girls in her country, she managed to become a superb writer. She became a crusading pen pal writing about the frustration of young Indonesian girls who had to stay at home and learn to do housework so that they could become good wives and mothers. Long after she died, the ideas in Kartini's letters were used to improve the system of education for girls in her country.

Malalai Joya is a young politician in the war-torn country of Afghanistan. She understands all too well that the women and girls in her country are denied the basic rights that are given to men and boys. Until very recently, Afghan girls have not been allowed to go to school, and are sometimes severely punished if they try to do so. As a member of her country's government, Malalai has tried to advocate for improved education for Afghanistan's girls and women, but most of the time she is met by extreme hostility, because powerful people want things to stay the same. Malalai's life is difficult: she must hide her face whenever she leaves her house because so many have threatened to silence her.

Finally, I've written about some exceptional women teachers who were lost to the world too young. Christa McAuliffe was an accomplished high school teacher who dreamed of traveling to space. By becoming the first teacher in space, she felt she could motivate young girls to reach for the stars, just as she had. Christa's life ended too soon, but her legacy of love for teaching lives on in the many schools and special programs that carry her name.

Friedl Dicker-Brandeis was a brilliant artist who lived during the inhuman period in history that we call the Holocaust. Even though she became a prisoner of the Nazis in a concentration camp, Friedl's extraordinary talent could not be stifled. Not only did she continue to make paintings herself, but she lovingly taught the imprisoned camp children to express their fears, hopes and desires through art. Friedl and many of her students did not survive the Holocaust, but their unforgettable and powerful pictures did.

I hope that you will enjoy discovering the stories of these ten very special women teachers. For all of them, teaching has been more than just a job; it has been a precious gift, which they have joyously shared with their students. Who knows: perhaps some day you may be inspired to do the same.

—Helen Wolfe

ONÉSIME DORVAL

Pioneer
Teacher

1845 - 1932

Many of us believe that speaking more than one language helps us to know our schoolmates and neighbors better. In the U.S., many people are bilingual because of the great numbers of Hispanic Americans. Spanish is very important and the language is taught in school. In Canada, many people are bilingual because of the Francophones (those who speak French as their first language) in Quebec and parts of other provinces. It makes sense that if we can speak each other's language, we can learn to appreciate each other's way of seeing the world. Nowadays there are lots of teachers who help students become bilingual. But until Onésime Dorval came along, there were few anywhere in North America.

Onésime Dorval was born into a Métis family in 1845, and grew up in the small town of St. Jerome, in Quebec, the Canadian province where most people speak French. The Métis' ancestors are a mix of two cultures: French and Aboriginal. They are one of the oldest cultural groups in Canada. After French explorers came to Canada in the sixteenth century, they were followed by settlers who established new colonies. Some of the French settlers who stayed in Canada married Aboriginal women. Their children and all of the other generations that followed are called Métis. There are still many Métis in Canada today. Onésime grew up understanding that she was a combination of two cultures, and she was proud of both.

Like many raised in Quebec at the time, Onésime was devoted to the Roman Catholic religion. As she was growing up, she developed a deep faith and dreamed that that she would spend her life serving people in need. But Onésime had a problem: her poor health. All through her childhood she was considered to be extremely frail. Most young girls at that time would have been content to accept this fact and stay quietly at home, cooking, sewing, and reading. But Onésime wanted to make a bigger difference in the world.

When she was a young woman in her twenties, Onésime made a life-changing decision. Her religious faith was so strong that she decided to become a nun. A nun gives up all of the possessions that most people wish for—a comfortable house, jewelry, or nice clothes—to lead a religious life. They focus completely on serving others. They also agree to sacrifice what most of us would consider to be a family life. Nuns don't get married or have children.

Once a woman decides to become a nun, she studies to prepare for a religious way of life. Women who aspire to be nuns are called novices, and live and study in a convent, which is a community of nuns. When Onésime was a novice, all nuns traded their clothes for a distinctive nun's habit, a long, loose black or gray dress, and a head covering that hid their hair completely. In those days, nuns usually cut their hair very short as well.

Onésime traveled to the United States to study to be both a teacher and a nun. In New York, she joined an order called the Sisters of the Good Shepherd. She lived and studied at the convent with the American nuns for a few years, and learned to speak English very well. Being bilingual in French and English was an unusual skill for a teacher of her time.

Novices make their vows three times after they enter their convents. They are observed by the community, and if all is well, they make their final vows and are accepted as nuns. To Onésime's huge disappointment, just when she was preparing to take her final vows, The Sisters of the Good Shepherd had bad news for her. One of her superiors had decided that she was too prone to illness, and wouldn't be strong enough to carry out the work. Onésime's dream of being a nun and teacher seemed to be dashed, and she was asked to leave the convent.

Although physically small and weak, Onésime was a deeply spiritual woman, and she still very much wanted to be a religious teacher. Instead of feeling sorry for herself, she asked around for opportunities. In due time she heard about

MAKING VOWS

When women become nuns, they make three important promises. These promises are called vows. Taking the vow of poverty means that a nun promises never to own or want anything valuable, like a house or a car. When she takes the vow of chastity, she is promising that she isn't going to have a man, or marriage, in her life. Finally, when a nun takes the vow of obedience, she promises to do whatever her superiors in the church tell her to, even if she sometimes might not want to.

a bishop from Saskatchewan named Vital Grandin, who was looking for women to do religious work in his home province. Saskatchewan, with its vast plains and small villages and towns, was pioneer country, where farmers grew wheat, barley, corn, and potatoes. Bishop Grandin of St. Albert, was looking for Roman Catholic women who were eager to set up missions (church schools) in Saskatchewan, and to work there as teachers.

In 1877, Onésime traveled to Saskatchewan to begin her missionary work. Her trip to this part of the country was long and difficult. The railroad which would one day span Canada was not yet built, so Onésime and her missionary friends made their way west on a Red River Cart—a large, simple wagon pulled by oxen, horses, or mules. They encountered lots of challenges on their way. Saskatchewan's flat terrain frequently causes its rivers to overflow when it rains, and the missionaries risked drowning as they crossed these cresting rivers in their Red River Cart, or rested for the night on a riverbank. They slept outside on the hard ground in all kinds of weather, and often ate spoiled food cooked on smoky campfires. The mosquitoes were fierce. For a frail, young woman like Onésime, the journey must have been exhausting. But her will kept her going.

Missionaries work hard and make many sacrifices. They sometimes find themselves in very remote, isolated places, and their lives can be uncomfortable or even dangerous. Before the era of cars and planes, missionaries like Onésime worked far from any cities or hospitals. They had to be very strong and self-reliant: if a missionary got sick or was in any other danger, there would be few people to help them in any way. Sometimes missionaries worked in places where they were not welcome, and would often risk their lives in the process.

For the first three years, Onésime worked as a missionary in all three prairie provinces of Canada: Manitoba,

Saskatchewan, and Alberta. She never stayed long in any one community or mission: after helping to set up a mission school in one town or village she'd then travel on to the next. One reason she was asked to move around so much was that she could teach and give religious education in both English and French. Being bilingual allowed her to communicate with the many Métis people in the area, whose mother tongue was French. Right from the start, Onésime was adored by everyone—French-speaking or English-speaking—for her gentle and joyful spirit.

The Métis people living near the missions were especially fond of her. She was one of them. She understood their culture and spoke French perfectly: no other teacher of theirs had done either before. Onésime was also beloved by the Métis for the respect she showed them. Most missionaries who came to the area had not dealt with the Métis kindly. They treated the Métis as if they were children, and made them feel they were not as good as everyone else. Many missionaries were strongly prejudiced against the Métis because they were part Aboriginal. They didn't respect the ancient Aboriginal cultures and ways of life. But Onésime was different. Because she was Métis herself, she treated her students and their families as equals. She was a humble, religious woman who never pretended that she was better than anyone else.

Onésime didn't just teach in the mission schools. She also decided to work as a housekeeper for some of the children she taught. Several of her students were very neglected. Their mothers had died, and they were being cared for by their hardworking fathers, who farmed in the fields from dawn to dusk. The men didn't have the time to cook, clean or make any kind of home for their kids. So Onésime devotedly made meals, dusted, swept, and sewed for her motherless students.

She also noticed that many of her students were walking very long distances to get to school every day, and that it was hard for them to get to classes during the long, icy winters. She gave these children the chance to live at the mission house where she herself lived. In that way, she could be sure that they'd be at school every day. Today, many students who attend private schools away from home live in school dorms with supervising teachers. But when Onésime was teaching, it was unheard of for mission students to live in the same house as their teacher. She was a kind, gentle, and motherly woman who went beyond the call of duty to ensure the happiness, health, and success of her students.

Onésime stayed longest—eighteen years, from 1896 to 1914—at the Saskatchewan mission school of St. Michael. At that time, quite a few school districts in North America covered vast areas of land with tiny populations. Teachers in these communities taught their students in one-room schoolhouses. The whole school was actually a big open room where all the students—from grade one to the end of high school—studied together with a single teacher. Teachers had to know all of the subjects for all of the grades. Onésime was one of these pioneers: she taught all the school subjects and gave religious education—in both English and French.

In 1921, after teaching in missions for forty-four years, Onésime Dorval finally retired, although she continued to do volunteer missionary work and wrote her memoirs. She did not return to Quebec, but instead decided to live permanently in Saskatchewan, the place she loved and now called home. She died on December 10, 1932, at the age of eighty-seven, and was buried in a cemetery beside St. Michael's School in Duck Lake. The woman who had not been able to become a nun because her health seemed too delicate, lived a long, energetic life of service to others.

The Canadian government has recognized the accomplishments of Onésime Dorval in important ways. Four small islands on her beloved North Saskatchewan River are now named after her. In 1954, she was named a person of national historical importance, and plaques were placed in her honor at several museums near her mission schools. She is remembered in Canadian history as one of the pioneer teachers in that part of the country—and the first who dedicated her life to creating a bilingual system of education.

ANNIE SULLIVAN MACY & HELEN KELLER

Opening the World's Eyes

ANNIE SULLIVAN MACY 1866 - 1936
HELEN KELLER 1880 - 1968

"How often have I been asked: 'If you had your life to live over, would you follow the same path? Would you be a teacher?' …. We do not, I think, choose our destiny. It chooses us." These are the words of Annie Sullivan Macy, who became the world-famous teacher of Helen Keller. With Annie's help, Helen overturned centuries of ignorance about the abilities of the deaf and blind.

It's almost a miracle that Annie Sullivan Macy survived her childhood. Annie (whose real name was Johanna) was born April 14, 1866 in Massachusetts. She was the oldest child of Thomas and Alice Cloesy Sullivan, who had emigrated to the United States from Ireland. Annie's family had little money, and faced harsh experiences in their new homeland. The Sullivans had five children, but two of them died when they were just babies. When she was five years old, Annie fell ill with a serious eye infection called trachoma, and it left her half blind. In those days, poor immigrant children suffered the worst consequences of illness, because their families couldn't afford doctors or even medicines.

When Annie was only eight, her mother died. While Annie's two surviving siblings were sent to live with relatives, she was expected to take care of her father because she was the oldest daughter. Life with Mr. Sullivan was frightening—he was an alcoholic and treated his young daughter brutally. When she grew up, Annie told stories of how her father shouted at her and beat her whenever he thought she'd done anything wrong.

Soon, Annie's living situation changed again, but not for the better. In 1876, when she was only ten years old, Annie and her younger brother Jimmie were sent to live at the Tewksbury Almshouse. An almshouse was a charitable home for poor children and adults who had no one to take care of them. Most of the children who lived there were orphans. A few, like Annie and her brother, were sent there because their mothers had died, and neither their fathers nor anyone else could take care of them.

The Tewksbury Almshouse was nothing like a family home. It was crowded and depressing. Girls and women, all strangers to each other, lived together in large, drafty wards or dormitories, separated from the men and boys. They were given poor food to eat and cast-off clothes to wear. There was no school for the children—nobody cared if they could read or write. Even worse, if someone got sick, there were no doctors, nurses, or medicines to help them. You had to be physically strong, have a tough character, and be able to take care of yourself to survive in an almshouse.

Luckily, ten-year-old Annie was able to cope, despite her

partial blindness. But she was worried about Jimmie, who was small, three years younger, and had problems walking because he had an incurable illness called tuberculosis. Although boys and girls in almshouses lived separately, big sister Annie somehow persuaded the director of Tewksbury to allow her to bring Jimmie to the women's section. He lived with her there, so that she could take care of him.

Many years later, Annie wrote about what it was like to live in the almshouse. She described Tewksbury as "cruel" and "indecent." She also wrote: "I was not shocked, pained, grieved, or troubled by what happened. People behaved like that—that was all that there was to it. It was all the life I knew. Things impressed themselves upon me because I had a receptive mind. Curiosity kept me alert and keen to know everything."

Annie's words tell us a lot about her personality. First of all, even though her life was difficult, she never felt sorry for herself. Annie was realistic and practical—she accepted her hardships and dealt with them as best she could. At the same time, she always kept her eyes and ears open and asked intelligent questions to help her cope. Being practical and observant helped Annie survive her challenging childhood. And these were the same traits that would make her the perfect teacher for Helen Keller in years to come.

Tragically, all of Annie's efforts as a big sister were not enough to help her brother. Jimmie died about six months after they arrived at Tewksbury. But even as she grieved, Annie stayed strong, determined to survive. Not long after her brother's death, Annie wandered into the small library at Tewksbury. She had never had the chance to go school, so she couldn't read or write. But being illiterate didn't stop this determined young girl. Annie was so hungry to learn that she persuaded people who were using the library to take the time to read to her. Before long, and with the help of a few kind souls, Annie began to read a bit by herself, despite her vision problems.

One day, when she was fourteen years old, an important visitor changed Annie's life. Frank Sanborn was the chairman of the state board of charities. Part of his job was to inspect the almshouse, to make sure that it was being run correctly. Annie recognized that he was someone who had the power to help her. As soon as she could, she ran to his side and, with great feeling, blurted out "Mr. Sanborn, I want to go to school!"

Her bold move worked. Soon, Annie left Tewksbury on her first train ride—to the Perkins Institution for the Blind in Boston, Massachusetts. Nowadays children with disabilities go to regular schools, where they can also have classes to help them with their special needs. In those days, children with disabilities were sent to separate schools, with other students who had the same handicaps.

Annie appreciated her chance to finally get an education, but she faced problems when she started going to the Perkins School. Even though she was fourteen, she knew far less than younger classmates. She became embarrassed when she couldn't spell the simplest words and her classmates laughed at her. The teachers at the Perkins School tried to create a warm, family atmosphere for their students, but Annie hadn't lived in a real family for a long time. She had never seen what it was like to get along with people, and to be polite when you asked for something. At the almshouse, Annie always had to fight hard for the things that she needed. She thought that the only way you could get anything was to be aggressive with people, so she behaved belligerently to her new classmates and teachers.

Annie had never owned so much as a comb for her hair or a nightgown to sleep in. When classmates teased her about how different she was, she would get into a temper. Sometimes, she'd angrily refuse to do her schoolwork, probably because she was unsure about how to do it, and too uncomfortable to ask for help. So Annie earned a reputation for being bad-tempered, and was nicknamed "Miss Spitfire" by the school director, Michael Anagnos. Although she had a rough start at the Perkins School, this man always believed in Annie. He was to become a very important person in her life.

Eventually, Annie got accustomed to her new surroundings, and started making excellent progress. Several teachers recognized her great intelligence and helped her to catch up to her classmates. Michael Anagnos boosted Annie's self-confidence by encouraging her to tutor younger students. She took another important step forward after she was able to have two eye operations, which improved her sight greatly. She had to wear thick reading glasses after her surgery, but didn't mind at all. Now she could read more rapidly and catch up to her classmates.

Some of the students at the school were both deaf and blind. One of the new things that Annie learned at the Perkins School was how to use the sign language alphabet to help kids who were both blind and deaf. Annie was a natural, and quickly became an expert sign language interpreter for the deaf-blind students. Little did she know what a key skill this would be in the not-too-distant future.

When she was twenty years old, Annie graduated from the Perkins Institution with high marks, and was chosen as the valedictorian of her graduating class. This special honor meant that Annie made a speech at her graduation before the whole school and invited guests. "Miss Spitfire" no more, Annie declared to her audience that day that being a student at Perkins had taught her to love truth, beauty, and goodness.

Around the time of Annie's graduation, Michael Anagnos, the school director and Annie's strong supporter, received a letter from a man named Arthur Keller.

One of Mr. Keller's three children was a little girl named Helen, who was almost seven years old. Helen had been a healthy, happy baby. But at nineteen months, she'd caught a

SIGNING THE ALPHABET

Each letter of the sign language alphabet has its own hand sign. When a person is deaf, she sees the hand signs and learns words that way. When a person is both deaf and blind and cannot see the signs, a sign language interpreter can help. The interpreter finger spells the words into the palm of her hand, one letter at a time, pausing between words. The deaf-blind person feels the signer's fingers moving inside her hand and can read the words.

brain disease called meningitis, and nearly died. After she'd recovered, Helen's parents realized that their little girl couldn't hear, see, or speak. Over the course of many years, Helen's family took her to numerous specialists to see if any of them could help their daughter. The answer from all the doctors was no. Helen Keller would remain blind, deaf, and mute for the rest of her life. The doctors also said that because Helen couldn't hear or see, she would never be able to learn anything. They told her parents that their daughter's situation was hopeless. It would be best if she went to live in an institution. According to the doctors, there was no point in keeping Helen at home or in sending her to school, because her disabilities made her unteachable.

The Kellers refused to accept that their little girl had such a bleak future, and they did not send her away. Now that Helen was of an age to start school, Captain Keller wrote to the Perkins Institution to seek a governess, a teacher who would be willing to live in the Kellers' house and give classes to the little girl at home. Michael Anagnos knew that teaching a child who was mute, blind, and deaf would be a huge challenge. All the same, he had faith that the intelligent and determined Annie Sullivan was exactly the right person to tackle this challenge head on.

On March 3, 1887, Annie Sullivan—who had just turned twenty-one—arrived at the Keller home in Alabama to begin working with Helen. From the first moment with her young student, Annie could see that there were many obstacles to teaching Helen. Looking at Helen was like looking in a mirror. In her new student, Annie saw some of the same uncontrolled behavior that she had displayed when she'd first arrived at the Perkins Institute. Helen was so stubborn that it was impossible to get her to do the simplest tasks, such as combing her hair, eating with a spoon, or learning to dress herself. In fact, in their early days together, Annie's lessons with Helen were more like wrestling matches. The teacher had to force her student to do these things against her will. Even though she could not speak, the seven-year-old threw huge, noisy temper tantrums.

Annie was keenly perceptive, and realized that working with Helen would be hard for two reasons. First of all, because she couldn't see, hear, or ask Annie questions, the little girl wasn't able to readily understand what Annie was trying to teach her. So it was natural that Helen would get confused and become frustrated with Annie. But there was another reason that she was so impatient, short-tempered, and uncooperative.

Helen had been allowed to run wild in the Keller home all of her life, always getting her own way. The Kellers believed that their daughter would never behave like a normal person, so they let her do whatever she wanted. Whenever Helen misbehaved, throwing food or knocking over her baby sister's highchair, the Kellers would just clean things up around her, and would never discipline her. They felt there was no point in disciplining Helen because she could not understand what she was doing wrong. And if Helen didn't get exactly what she wanted, she would have temper tantrums, kicking and stamping her feet like a baby.

Helen Keller

Annie believed that the problem was simple— Helen was just a spoiled

Helen Keller and Annie Sullivan in 1897

brat. Even though she couldn't see or hear, she was still a smart child, who needed to be disciplined if she misbehaved. Annie thought that Helen should be treated just like any other child. Only a week after she arrived in the Keller home, Annie realized that she had to work with Helen away from the family. She thought that this was necessary to get Helen to trust and obey her. Because she wasn't a relative, she wasn't so emotionally attached, and wouldn't let Helen get away with her wild behavior so easily.

Annie persuaded the Kellers to allow her and Helen to move into a small garden house on the family property, away from the big house. Annie made the Kellers a deal. First, she promised them that if she could be alone with Helen for just two weeks, she would be able to teach her student the basic life skills that she had never learned. In that time Helen would start to dress and feed herself, just like other little girls her age. But Annie's most important promise to the Kellers was that she would be able to tame Helen's unruly behavior. Annie claimed that because they would be all alone, Helen would have to depend on her for everything—she wouldn't have any choice but to do what her teacher asked. Annie promised that in two weeks, the Keller family would have a calm, well-behaved child. Her temper tantrums would be gone forever.

During their two weeks in the garden house, Annie kept both her promises. She was able to show Helen that learning things step by step and being patient was much better than throwing a tantrum. Annie was elated that Helen was becoming a calmer child and beginning to trust her teacher. Helen learned to eat with a spoon and to dress herself. She also learned to control her temper.

Secretly, Annie was also hoping for another important breakthrough in Helen's education. As soon as she'd arrived in the Keller home, Annie had begun to teach Helen sign language, using the method that she had learned for deaf-blind people. From almost the first moment that they met, Annie began to spell letters and words into Helen's hand. Every time Helen touched an object or did any action, Annie would spell the word for it into Helen's palm. In the beginning, Annie knew that this "finger spelling" was only a game to Helen. Annie would spell words into Helen's hand, and Helen copied her by spelling the same words back into her hand. Annie was pleased, but she wasn't sure that Helen understood that the words she was spelling meant anything.

While they were alone in the garden house, Annie continued spelling hundreds of words into Helen's hands. As they walked around the little garden house, Annie would have her student touch things: a chair, a table, or some flowers. Each time Helen touched an object, her teacher would then finger spell the name of the object into Helen's hand. Annie would use the same method to teach Helen the signs for actions like "playing," "dancing," and "walking." Annie could only hope that if she repeated the finger spelling over and over again, Helen would eventually make the connection between the sign language and the words that it represented. Helen would finally understand that words had meanings.

When their two weeks alone in the garden house were almost over, something wonderful happened. On their last walk in the garden, they stopped by a water pump. Annie pumped water into her student's hand, just as she had done many times during the last two weeks. As Helen was touching the water with one hand, Annie signed the word for water into her other hand. Helen spelled the word back to her teacher, her usual reaction. Annie took Helen around to different parts of the garden and the little house, letting Helen touch everything around her. But this time Annie let Helen touch many things, and didn't automatically finger spell their names into Helen's hand. Instead, the teacher waited for her student to touch something and then finger spell its name all by herself. Annie knew that if Helen could finger spell the words for the things that she touched, then she must know what the words meant. It worked! Helen did finger spell the correct words, dozens of them, hundreds of them, into Annie's hand. She really did know what these words meant!

Annie knew that this was a giant step in teaching Helen Keller to communicate with the world. Helen and Annie's first weeks together, and Helen's breakthrough to understanding the meaning of words, have become very famous. Their story was later celebrated in a hugely popular play and then in a multi-award-winning movie, both called *The Miracle Worker*.

Once she made this extraordinary breakthrough, Helen learned very rapidly. After only a year, Annie and Helen visited the Perkins School. Everyone was astounded at how much Helen could do. Not only was she learning a very high level of language, but, with Annie's help, she was even starting to speak. Michael Anagnos was so impressed that he spread the word about Annie and Helen to important people such as Alexander Graham Bell, the inventor of the telephone. Bell and other wealthy supporters gave Helen and Annie money so that Helen could attend excellent schools, and learn even more.

Helen Keller and
Annie Sullivan in 1913

When Helen Keller was only ten years old, she was enrolled at Radcliffe, a top college for the brightest women. Annie and her student sat together in the classroom with the others, and worked together as a team. Annie would listen to the professor's lecture and then use finger spelling to communicate the ideas to Helen. Annie read the textbooks, took notes, and communicated what was in them to Helen. This partnership worked so well that Helen graduated with honors from Radcliffe College when she was only fourteen years old.

Another life-changing event for them occurred at Radcliffe. There, Annie and Helen met John Macy, a teacher who helped them to create Helen's autobiography. The book was titled *My Life*, and was published some years later, when Helen was twenty-two years old. While they were working together on the story of Helen's life and accomplishments, Annie and John fell in love and got married. Annie, Helen, and John decided to live in one big house.

But this unusual family of three was never a comfortable one. By then, Helen and Annie were very famous. They were away from home a lot, traveling and giving speeches about Helen's story, and trying to earn enough to support three people. As a result, Annie and John never got to spend much time together as a married couple. The fees for speeches and John's income were not quite enough for their living and travel expenses, so money was a constant problem. To add to their troubles, Annie's eyesight was getting worse, and

Helen Keller and President Coolidge in 1926

she developed tuberculosis, the illness that had killed her little brother. It's not surprising that Annie sometimes suffered from depression because she was overwhelmed by her problems. In the end, after being married for nine years, Annie and John decided that they had to separate, and he moved away to England. They did not divorce, but never lived together again.

Annie and Helen stayed in the same house for the rest of Annie's life. When Annie felt well enough, the two of them traveled and made speeches about the need for deaf-blind people to get a good education. Annie and Helen even went to Hollywood and made a silent movie called *Deliverance*, based on their life stories. They also created a stage act for vaudeville, a popular form of entertainment in the early 1900s. In the end, Helen and Annie raised more than two million dollars for the Helen Keller Endowment Fund to educate deaf-blind people. It was a phenomenal achievement.

Annie Sullivan Macy died in 1936 at the age of seventy, with Helen by her side. Although she was then without her beloved teacher, Helen continued making speeches championing the rights of deaf and blind people. In fact, she was able to do that for the rest of her very long life. Helen Keller died in 1968 at the age of 87.

These two exceptional women are not with us anymore, but their contributions have made a huge mark on history. Today, people who are deaf or blind, or both, lead very different lives from those of Helen Keller and Annie Sullivan Macy. Of course, many still face challenges in getting a good education and having access to other rights that everyone else takes for granted. But because of Annie and Helen, their days have been immeasurably brightened. We recognize people with special needs as our family, friends, classmates and neighbors, who enjoy life with the rest of us.

MARIA MONTESSORI

The
Student
Comes
First

1870 - 1952

Before Maria Montessori came along, there was basically one way to teach. Teachers would lecture, while the kids sat listening in their rows of desks, hands quietly folded in their laps. The only learning materials in the classroom were books, paper, pencils, and pens—maybe a roll-down map near the blackboard. But some students just can't learn in classes like that. It might take them longer than others to understand their teacher, or they might be too restless to sit at their desks for long stretches of time. Maria Montessori was unique because she observed that not all children learn in the same ways. Today, many of the everyday things we do in classrooms, and take for granted, are a result of Maria's realization. And there are thousands of Montessori schools using her methods all over the world.

Maria Montessori didn't start out wanting to be a teacher. She was born into a well-off family in Chiaravalle, Italy, on August 31, 1870. Her father, Alessandro, a government official, was an army officer before his daughter was born, and had quite traditional ideas. But Maria's mother, Renilde, was a modern, forward-looking woman, who taught her daughter to have compassion for people in need. When Maria was still very young, Renilde showed her how to knit, and encouraged her to make clothing for charity. The Montessori family had servants to clean their house, but Maria knew from her mother that most people cleaned their houses by themselves. The little girl was curious and wanted to understand how that felt, so she decided to wash part of the kitchen floor every single day. Although Maria was born into in a privileged family, she grew up sympathizing with people who were not as fortunate. She also learned an appreciation for hard work.

In elementary school, Maria did not stand out as an especially talented student. Actually, her teachers thought that she was of average intelligence. But she always worked hard, did well in her exams, and was a lively class leader who invented games for everyone to play. Maria later confessed that she was bored in school, because the lessons and tests were so repetitious. Doing the same dry exercises over and over, and memorizing pages of facts, was not a joy for her. She didn't much like being in school, but because she was bright she learned quickly.

When it was time for her to leave elementary school, Maria's parents had to make an important decision. Her father and mother disagreed about their daughter's education. Her father, in his traditional way of thinking, wanted Maria to end her schooling and start preparing herself for her eventual marriage. But Maria's mother rejoiced that her daughter was creative and intelligent, and she had very different ideas. She was eager for Maria to have a career, and wanted her to continue with her education. Maria's mother had always had great influence on the family's decisions. Maria would continue her studies.

At age thirteen, Maria decided that she wanted to know more about math and engineering, and enrolled at a technical institute. At that time, girls did not study these subjects, and Maria was the only female student in the school. Gradually, she became keenly interested in other areas of science. When Maria took a course in human biology, the science of how our bodies work, she decided to become a doctor, something almost unheard of for women of the time. She was turned down three years in a row by the University of Rome's medical school. No Italian woman had ever attempted this before, but eventually Maria's persistence paid off, and she was able to begin her medical studies.

When she was twenty-four years old, Maria graduated

GIRLS AND SCHOOL

In Europe of the late 1800s, girls usually competed their formal education at about age twelve. Most people believed that it was enough for girls to learn how to read and write and to understand some mathematics. After elementary school, girls from poor families went to work in factories or shops, or as servants in rich households. Girls from wealthier families like Maria's usually stayed at home or went to "finishing school" to learn what were called "domestic skills." Young ladies learned manners, perhaps how to draw or play a musical instrument, and how to cook, clean, and sew, because they were expected to get married and manage everything in their own homes. At that time, it was unusual for a girl to go to high school or university.

from medical school, and became the first woman doctor in Italy. She earned the title Dottoressa, which means "female doctor" in Italian—a title that stuck with her the rest of her life. Dottoressa Montessori's first job was at the University of Rome, where she worked with mentally disabled patients. Here, Maria met children who had problems learning things—children we would consider to have "special needs" today. It was hard for them to dress themselves or to learn how to read. Nowadays, there are many students with special needs in classes with "regular kids," and teachers don't focus on the things that they can't do. Kids with special needs participate in classroom activities and get extra help to do the things that everyone else does. But when Maria was treating these children, they were called "hopelessly deficient" or even "idiots." At that time, kids with special needs didn't go to school. Instead, they were patients in hospitals or clinics. Doctors thought that children with learning challenges had illnesses that might be helped with medicines or other therapies.

As Maria started to work with her new patients, she observed that they did learn new things, despite what everyone said. She became convinced that these kids were not sick. They didn't need medicine or treatment, just a different kind of teaching. She believed that children with special needs could learn very well, using methods that no one had ever tried to use before. After she'd tried a few ideas with them, Maria saw that kids with special needs learned best when they could use their five senses: tasting, touching, smelling, hearing, and seeing.

One of Maria's favorite sayings was: "First the education of the senses, then the education of the intellect (using your intelligence)." Doesn't that kind of teaching seem familiar to you? Isn't playing and having experiences by touching, seeing, and hearing the way that you learned new words when you were in daycare or kindergarten? As you can see, Maria

Montessori's teaching methods aren't just used in Montessori schools, but in the daycares and schools that all kids attend.

After a few highly successful years teaching children with special needs, Maria was offered another challenge. The government put her in charge of a new public school in a very run-down part of Rome called San Lorenzo. The name of the school was Casa dei Bambini (Children's House) and it was a preschool for underprivileged kids. There were sixty students, from three to six years old, all from very poor families. Maria decided that since her ideas had worked with special needs kids, she might as well try the same method with these younger students. She started teaching them using the activities she'd invented, and soon added even more new ideas.

As she watched the children playing, it became obvious to her that they learned well when they were allowed to explore and be active. She taught them games where they moved around, got lots of exercise, and improved their co-ordination. She also used puzzles to keep learning fun for the kids. She had the older children teach the younger ones skills that they had already learned. In this way, the older students became

INSIDE MARIA'S IDEAS

Imagine you were a child with reading difficulties who could not read the word "sand." Using Maria Montessori's ideas, you wouldn't learn the word by merely trying to read it or sound it out. Instead, your teacher would let you play with sand for a long time—touching it, smelling it, and maybe building a sandcastle with it. Your teacher would give you lots of time to play with the sand in many different ways. Finally, your teacher would read a story about sand with you. You would read the word out loud with her, and then remember it. Later on, you might even write a story using that word. This was a foundation of the Montessori method.

teacher's helpers as well as role models for the younger students. Doesn't that sound similar to peer teaching in our schools today? She also decided to change the way that the classroom was set up. Gone were the traditional rows of desks. In Maria's school, the desks were replaced by tables and chairs, with a lot of space around them so that the students could move around freely.

Although many of Maria's students were too little to go to a regular school, they were still learning a lot of language. To help them, she created a set of 3-D letters that the kids could hold, play with, and put together to make words. She also figured out a similar way to help children understand numbers, using blocks, beads, and other objects that they

Maria Montessori used "play and learn" activities in her classes.

could play with to practice their counting and early math. All the "play and learn" activities we see in daycare centers and kindergartens today are like the ones Maria invented for her children more than a hundred years ago.

News of her interesting new teaching ideas spread. But many Italian teachers were actually a little frightened by them. They were used to their students obediently sitting in rows of desks, doing their classwork with pencils and paper. Perhaps they worried that this new kind of classroom would be too noisy, and that they might have discipline problems with the students. The administrators of the public schools said that children would not be able to learn much unless their teacher tightly controlled them. Maria was sure that they were all wrong. She had seen how children learned best when they enjoyed their activities. They became more eager to learn—and learned so much more—when they had freedom, play, and variety.

Maria became frustrated that her ideas weren't being accepted in Italy, so she decided to travel to other countries to let teachers know about the Montessori method. In 1913, she made her first visit to the United States, where she met the inventor of the telephone, Alexander Graham Bell, and his wife Mabel. The Bells became real supporters of Maria's methods, and founded the Montessori Education Association at their home in Washington, D.C. Maria also got encouragement from the inventor Thomas Edison, and from the extraordinary Helen Keller.

Two years later, she attracted attention all over the world with a special project at the International Exhibition in San Francisco. There Maria created a classroom with glass walls. In this classroom, about twenty children carried on their school day according to the Montessori Method. As in Maria's other classrooms, there were no rows of desks or structured lessons. Visitors to this unusual exhibit could observe the students

Dr. Sam McClure wrote of Maria's methods in his U.S.
magazine, McClure, and in 1914 persuaded her to visit the
U.S. where her methods were taking root.

exploring, experimenting, and learning language and math Maria's way. Here was the Montessori method in action for all to see, and it became a sensation. During the next ten years, Maria traveled to England, Spain, and Holland, where she talked about her methods and gave courses to teachers. Maria had a mission: she wanted to persuade teachers everywhere that allowing children to explore and to experience new things would help them to learn faster and understand better. More and more people started to see things Maria's way: instead of being a blank page for others to write on, each child's mind was full of potential, waiting to be released by the right activities and surroundings.

Her reputation soared. When Maria eventually returned to Italy, the Italian government made her the official inspector of schools. This job meant that she would travel around the country to see what was going in the schools. She could then make suggestions to teachers about improving their lessons so that all of the students could learn in better ways.

But trouble and changes were in the air. In the 1920s and 30s, the government in Italy came under the leadership of a repressive dictator named Benito Mussolini. Mussolini, and the German dictator Adolf Hitler, were preparing to invade countries all over Europe. Mussolini was building a huge army for this purpose. He wanted to open special schools to train the soldiers. He asked Maria to create those army training schools, and to be in charge of them. Maria made up her mind that she would never be part of this dictator's plan. It was a difficult decision, but by 1934 Maria knew that it was time to leave her homeland. Hitler's and Mussolini's rise to power and invasion of many European countries led to World War II, which actually began in 1939.

First, Maria immigrated to Spain, but a civil war broke out there in 1936. Then, she traveled to other countries in Europe, hoping to persuade even more teachers that the Montessori method was better for students than their traditional ways of teaching. She visited Holland, and opened the first Montessori Training Center for teachers. From there, she went on to Sri Lanka and India with her grown-up son Mario, to open up another teacher training center. The Indian authorities got the mistaken idea that Maria was on the side of Mussolini and Hitler, so she and her son were actually put in prison for a short time. After they were released, Maria was allowed to continue with her training courses. She created a Montessori Centre in London, England in 1947, only two years after the end of the war.

For the last few years of her life, Maria lived in Holland. In 1949, 1950, and 1951, she was nominated for an extremely important honor, the Nobel Peace Prize. The Nobel Peace Prize is a special award, given for making an enormous contribution to the world. Although Maria never actually received it, just being nominated for the award showed the size of her achievements.

Maria Montessori died in Holland in 1952, at the age of 82. Her son carried on with her work, speaking about the Montessori method and helping to open Montessori schools for the rest of his life.

Montessori schools are still popular all over the world: in the United States alone, there are more than 3,000. Many of Maria's key ideas, such as learning through the senses, group activities, and peer learning, are universally used in today's schools—whether they are Montessori schools or not. Her ideas about education have changed the way that a classroom looks, and the ways that kids are taught, everywhere. Perhaps her greatest contribution was to understand how to bring out the very best in every child—even those that the world had given up on. Maria gave them the joy of learning.

RADEN AYU KARTINI

Indonesian
National
Hero

1879 - 1904

The island nation of Indonesia is located in Southeast Asia, near Vietnam and Thailand. U.S. President Barack Obama spent part of his childhood in Indonesia, the home of his stepfather. The island of Java, one of the largest Indonesian islands, was the birthplace of Raden Ayu Kartini, a fascinating Javanese noblewoman.

She lived during the time that the Dutch ruled her country, more than 150 years ago. Kartini had a very short life, but she is a hero to the people of Indonesia to this day. Though she never managed to fulfill her own dream of becoming a teacher, she helped young girls and women in her country achieve the right to education, during a time when this was considered revolutionary. In her brief lifetime, Kartini became known as a trailblazer for women's rights, especially for the women of Indonesia.

Raden Ayu Kartini was born on April 21, 1879, into an aristocratic family, which meant that she would lead a comfortable and privileged life. She grew up in a lavish Indonesian house compound built around a courtyard. There were dozens of servants to take care of the housework and to provide Kartini with anything she wanted or needed. Hardships and struggles were never part of her experience.

Kartini was one of the many children of Raden Mas Sosroningrat, who was a member of the government, as well as holder of the noble title of Regency Chief of Jepara. Her father, a devout Muslim, had more than one wife, which was customary for Muslim men at the time. Kartini's mother was her father's first wife, but she wasn't a member of the nobility. Kartini's father married his second wife for her family's noble line. According to custom, he had to marry an aristocrat in order to maintain his title of Regent.

WHAT'S IN A NAME?

In Europe and many other places, royal and noble families have titles like Sir, Lady, Duke, or Duchess, that go before their names. In Java too, titles were given to every member of an aristocratic family. Kartini, her father, and other Javanese aristocrats had the title Raden, which went before their family names to show their high birth.

Kartini was her father's fifth child, and the second oldest daughter of a family with eleven children in total. When she was a little girl, she was full of energy, and loved to play outdoors and climb trees. In fact, she was given the nickname "little bird," because one of her favorite games was to spread her arms out and pretend she was flying around. She never seemed to sit still.

At the time that Kartini was growing up, in the late 1800s, it was very unusual for little Indonesian girls to be educated. But her father was more liberal than most, and allowed his daughter to go to a Dutch elementary school along with her brothers. Going to a school, let alone one where everyone spoke Dutch, was a privilege that most Javanese girls of the time could never have dreamed possible. But Kartini had that chance, because her family was rich and important.

Her family allowed her to attend this school until she was twelve years old, and she did very well. Kartini learned to speak, read, and write Dutch fluently, something very rare for a girl of her culture. The fact that she could speak more than one language became very important later on in her life.

After she turned twelve, Kartini was taken out of school and had to remain at home, in seclusion. This custom, called *pingit*, was a part of Islam, the religion of Kartini and her family, as practiced in Java. At that time, being secluded at home until marriage was normal for young Javanese girls. Spending the days learning how to cook, clean, sew, and take care of a house and children, Kartini and other girls rarely left their houses until their fathers arranged a suitable marriage for them—usually to someone they had never met.

Once Indonesian girls got married, they had to ask their husbands for permission to do anything, especially for an activity that would take them outside their homes. So, during Kartini's time women had little control over their own lives, right from the time they were born. All of the power their fathers had over them as girls passed into the hands of their husbands.

During her seclusion, Kartini's father was more open and understanding than most fathers of that time. He allowed her to have certain privileges such as taking embroidery lessons, and he let her go out in public to attend special events. Kartini was an intelligent and curious young girl, and she continued to read books and to educate herself as well as she could. Because she could speak Dutch, she had several Dutch friends, and she wrote letters to them. They happily wrote back.

Nowadays, because we have Facebook, Twitter and other social networking sites, people can communicate with their friends all over the world easily, quickly, and in real time. But in Kartini's day, sharing thoughts and ideas with a distant friend was different—a letter could take weeks to get to its destination, and then it would take weeks more to get an answer. But despite this, over the course of many years her pen pals helped Kartini break through the walls of her seclusion, and allowed her to reach out to the world beyond her father's house. She had one especially close friend named Rosa Abendanon. Kartini and Rosa had met and become friends in school, and when they were separated, they poured out their thoughts and feelings to each other in frequent long letters.

As she matured, Kartini wrote to Rosa and her other European pen pals about some things that bothered her, including the lack of freedom for women and girls in Java. Rosa became Kartini's link to new ideas to help women, ideas that people in Holland and the rest of Europe were talking about. Kartini wrote to her faraway friends that the people of Java needed better education in order to enjoy better lives. In many of her letters she pointed out how Javanese girls and women in particular had limited horizons and few choices. She didn't understand why girls in her culture needed to hide themselves in their parents' homes. And why were the rich boys in her culture encouraged to study, so that they could be whatever they wanted to be, while poor people—and especially girls—had no chance for the same dreams?

At the time Kartini started writing to her European friends, people in Europe and America were starting to discuss how girls and women could improve their lives. Europeans were beginning to accept that girls and women should be equal with men. Women should be able to vote and get the highest level of education that they could—even attend college or university to become doctors, lawyers, writers, or whatever they wanted to be. Kartini's pen pals passed these new developments along to their friend in Java. Their letters opened a whole new world of possibilities to her. Her good friend Rosa sent her books, newspapers, and magazines. These Kartini devoured, and they opened her eyes even more to all the ways that girls and women in Java could have better lives.

For the first time, Kartini began to feel that new winds were blowing in her life. She started to question her father's right to keep her and her sisters in seclusion, unable to have the same opportunities as her brothers and other boys. Although he loved her—and allowed her to read Dutch books and correspond with her friends abroad—Kartini's father did not approve of her new ideas at all. He was more liberal than many, but still believed that such freedoms were unsuitable for girls. He worried that Kartini wouldn't be happy if she kept pursuing these strange thoughts.

Besides, time had passed and Kartini was already twenty-four years old. She was in no hurry to get married, and her father became concerned that she would never find a husband. Most Javanese girls her age were married, with several children. To aristocratic people in her culture, Kartini was already considered too old to marry a rich and powerful young man. Her father may have thought that enough was enough—she needed to be married quickly.

When she was twenty-four, her parents arranged a marriage to Raden Adpati Joyoadiningrat. He was a fifty-year-old man who already had three wives and twelve children. Kartini had been thinking about becoming a teacher. In fact, she had been awarded a scholarship to study in Europe, but this arranged marriage meant that she had to turn the scholarship

ARRANGED MARRIAGE

Arranged marriage is a custom that is still practiced today in some cultures. The idea behind the custom is that the parents of a young man or woman are older and wiser than their children. It follows that it should be their responsibility to choose partners for their children to marry. Parents who arrange their children's marriages think carefully about their children's personalities, likes and dislikes, and try to choose the right partners for them. Young people who have this cultural belief respect their parents and trust that a good partner will be picked out for them.

down. Even though she was disappointed and unhappy that her life was not in her control, Kartini felt she was obliged to obey her father.

On November 12, 1903, Kartini married the man of her father's choice. And soon after, she had quite a happy surprise. Her husband actually supported her ideas, and she soon found that her dream of offering Javanese girls an education would come true after all. Her new husband immediately used his influence with the Dutch government to help Kartini open the first primary school for Javanese girls. What was important to her was that any Javanese girl could go to this school, whether rich or poor. The small school, which was situated inside her father's house, taught reading, handicrafts, and the Muslim religion to girls and young women. Kartini created a guide for the teachers in her school, with a variety of ideas for teaching girls and women who had had little or no formal education before.

Sadly, both Kartini's life and her career as an educator were extremely brief. On September 17, 1904, Kartini died while giving birth to her first child. She was just twenty-five.

After her death, the letters that she had sent to her Dutch

friends in Europe were published—first as a book in Holland, and later in English as *Letters of a Javanese Princess*. Her published letters changed the way that the Dutch people, who ruled Indonesia, thought about and treated Javanese women and girls. They saw through her eyes the injustice of Javanese women and girls having scarcely any choices, and no freedom to learn and study. Her letters also exposed the plight of Javanese women who, by custom, had to marry men they did not know, men who already had other wives. Some of them were decent husbands who treated their wives well, but many

Kartini with her husband, Joyoadiningrat

were unjust and treated their wives like slaves. Kartini passionately criticized the fact that Muslim men could have more than one wife. She believed that this practice was unfair to women, and kept them from becoming independent, and equal to the men in her country. Through her letters, Kartini was able to express the sadness and frustration that she could not openly talk about while she was alive.

In one very special letter, she wrote that the world would be more peaceful if people didn't use religion as a reason to have disagreements and start wars. In her words: "Religion must guard us against committing sins, but more often, sins are committed in the name of religion." Unfortunately, throughout history many terrible things have happened because of religious differences. Kartini's ideas ring just as true now as when they were written.

As more and more people read her letters, many in Java and all over Asia became inspired by Kartini's ideas. Admirers

IN HER OWN WORDS

Throughout her lifetime, Kartini continually demonstrated her thirst for more freedom and experience through her letter writing. She wrote these lines to a Dutch pen pal when she was 20 years old.

" I have been longing to make the acquaintance of a modern girl, that proud independent girl who has all my sympathy! She who, happy and self reliant, lightly and alertly steps her way through life; full of enthusiasm and warm feelings; working not only for her own well-being and happiness, but for the greater good of humanity as a whole."

From *Letters of a Javanese Princess* – Raden Ayu Kartini's letters in Java established "Kartini schools," where local girls and women could get some kind of education for the first time in their lives. In 1945, Indonesia won independence from Holland and from then on was governed by its own Constitution, a document that guaranteed the rights of freedoms of all Indonesians. In it, Indonesian women were promised the same rights as men—to vote in elections and to have access to education and career opportunities.

BEING A PEN PAL

Pen pals or pen friends are people who regularly write to each other. People often have pen pals in other countries so that they can practice reading and writing in languages other than their first languages. Since the Internet was invented, it has been easy to become a pen pal and to communicate with "friends" all over the world in "real time."

But, for hundreds of years before the Internet existed, people just like Raden became pen pals by simply starting to write letters to each other, and mailing the letters to faraway places. For many young women like Kartini, who could never dream of traveling away from their home countries, becoming a pen pal to one or many people was their window to the world. They could share their thoughts and ideas, read about new ones, and carry on friendships that would last a lifetime. Even today, we can learn more about the innermost thoughts of feelings of many great people through their letters.

Nowadays, you can find a pen pal almost anywhere in the world. But make sure that you get guidance from your teacher, local religious organization, or community center. There are also websites that can show you how to become a pen pal, but always make sure that your parents, teachers, or another adult that you trust helps you to get started.

April 21, Kartini's birthday, is now a national holiday, when everyone in Indonesia recognizes her as a pioneer for women's rights and the freedom to make choices. During the holiday, Indonesian women and girls wear the traditional clothes that she would have worn, to show their respect. Mothers are allowed the day off, and the men in the family do the cooking and the housework.

On this day, Indonesian students discuss her achievements, and women's organizations organize parades in her honor. An Indonesian filmmaker made a popular movie about Kartini's life, ambitions, and her contribution to Indonesia. She is still an inspiration, even beyond her homeland. Kartini International, an organization based in Canada—nearly 10,000 miles away from Java—helps women from many cultures secure equal rights and better education.

Raden Ayu Kartini lived and wrote at a time when most women had few choices, and little control over their lives. If we look at the severe limitations of her life, it would be easy to think of her as a victim, but the opposite is true. Because of her extraordinary intelligence and eagerness to learn new ideas, she became a pioneer in women's education and equal rights in her country. And she inspired thousands around the world to carry on her work, long after her short life ended.

FRIEDL DICKER-BRANDEIS

Light in the Darkness

1890 - 1944

Some girls realize that they want to teach when they grow up, and this becomes their dream and goal. But others, like artist Friedl Dicker-Brandeis, become teachers because outside forces bring them to this calling. History changed Friedl's life, and made her a loving and brilliant teacher in the most heartbreaking of circumstances.

Friedl Dicker was born into a poor Jewish family in Vienna, Austria in 1898. Her mother, Karolina, died when Friedl was just four years old. Her father, Simon, did his best to raise his little girl on his own, and helped her deal with the loneliness of being motherless. Mr. Dicker worked at a stationery store and sold paper and art supplies, such as paints, brushes, and colored pencils. He wanted his daughter to explore her creativity, so he brought home armloads of art supplies from the store. All through her childhood, Friedl spent long hours happily painting and experimenting with different styles of art.

By the time she was a teenager, her father could see that Friedl had a special gift, and would benefit from formal art lessons. So, at thirteen, she began studying graphic arts at the Experimental School of Graphics in Vienna.

Friedl was never satisfied exploring just one particular style of graphic art. She loved to experiment with many styles and genres. Ever curious, she took up textile design at the Viennese Royal School of Applied Arts. Textile design is the art of patterning fabrics such as cotton or silk with woven designs or embroidery. The results can be made into clothing, used on furniture, or hung on a wall, like a painting. She showed such talent that she was accepted at a famous German school called the Bauhaus, and there she studied art and design with notable modern artists. When she was only twenty-one, Friedl and a good friend started their own bookbinding business. Most books are bound in paper, by factory machines. But at that time, handcrafted books were prized, and artists would make unique book covers out of leather and cloth. Friedl's

GRAPHIC ARTS

The look of books, magazines, or websites, the patterns on sheets and clothes, the logos on packaging and products—all these are created by graphic artists. Today, many graphic artists use software to create their designs digitally. But when Friedl was studying graphic arts, she designed with pencils, rulers, charcoal, and paintbrush on paper. She experimented with printing techniques, and learned how to use a camera in her photography classes.

outstanding talents were recognized by the Bauhaus school, and she was given the honor of teaching the freshman art class. Some of Friedl's students were no older than she was.

Friedl had an adventurous spirit, and never worried about taking chances. In 1923, after teaching for a few years at the Bauhaus, Friedl and her friend Franz Singer opened up a business called the Workshops for Visual Arts, where they sold textiles, books, and jewelry of their own design. After that, she returned to her home in Vienna with Franz and opened the Atelier Singer-Drucker, which they built into one of the most highly regarded design businesses in the city, selling art and furniture of their own creation, and even designing buildings. She continued to draw and paint, becoming one of the well-known young artists in Vienna. Through her business activities, Friedl became involved with education again when she designed a Montessori kindergarten. She believed that teachers should use art to inspire creativity in kids, so she started teaching art to kindergarten teachers.

Friedl believed that people should be free to express themselves and live any way they wish, as long as they didn't harm other people. She held strong opinions, and wasn't afraid to voice them openly.

Like many other artists of her time, she joined the Communist Party, a political group who believed that governments should provide for everyone's needs equally, and that private businesses—where a few people could become wealthy while others remained poor—are unjust. The Austrian government, along with many others, thought that the Communists were a danger to their country. In 1934, Friedl was arrested for her Communist activities, and put in prison for a short time.

After her release, Friedl fled to live in the beautiful city of Prague, in Czechoslovakia (now the Czech Republic). There, she fell in love with and married one of her cousins, an accountant named Pavel Brandeis. During this time, from 1934 to 1938, Friedl started looking for a way to earn extra money. She began to teach art to the sons and daughters of German people who had decided to leave Germany where the hate campaigns of the Nazi Party were accelerating. Although she had never intended to be a teacher, Friedl's students loved her because she was so inspiring and warm. Many felt that she treated them like a mother would.

Though the storm clouds of war were gathering, Friedl and her husband continued to live with relative freedom in Prague. But in Germany, where she had worked and studied, the government was making it almost impossible for many to live and work. Adolf Hitler and his followers, the Nazis, were taking away the basic freedoms of many German citizens. There were groups of people that Hitler targeted as dangerous, and the Nazis now had the power to pass laws that made these people prisoners in Germany. Two of the groups singled out were Jews and the Communists. Now Hitler was recruiting his followers into a huge, powerful army, and wanted to conquer all of Europe.

Friedl's friends and fellow artists began to hear rumors of terrible things that were happening to Jews and Communists in Germany. Although she wasn't especially religious, Friedl was Jewish, and like many in her circle, a Communist. Many of her friends decided that it was too dangerous to stay in Central Europe, and decided to leave before it was too late. They abandoned their homes and emigrated to England, North America, and South America, where people were free to live as they wished. Friedl obtained a passport and special permission to go to Palestine, but in the end, Friedl would not leave her husband behind. She and Pavel decided to stay, believing that since they were not in Germany, Hitler and the Nazis had no power to harm them.

But the couple did think that it would be safer to start

fresh in a place where no one knew about their religion or their political beliefs. They moved to the small town of Hronov, where they both found jobs in a textile factory. However, Friedl and Pavel found little safety there. Word of Nazi power and Hitler's army had spread. They were forced to move from one apartment to another several times, when fearful landlords discovered that they were both Jewish and Communists. They both kept losing their jobs for the same reasons. This difficult way of life went on for several years, until 1942.

By this time, the German army had invaded and occupied many countries in Europe, including Czechoslovakia. When one country occupies another, they take over the running of the country and make laws that fit their own ambitions. So, in Czechoslovakia in 1942, Jews, Communists, and other groups were singled out. They were watched by the Nazi authorities, and were not allowed to travel or cross the border. They weren't allowed to go out after dark, so they couldn't see their friends, go to movies, or to restaurants. But most frightening of all was a new development. Now Jews, Communists, and others that Hitler had targeted were being ordered out of their homes, and deported to bleak, inhumane prison camps, called concentration camps.

This time in history when Hitler and the Nazis were trying to conquer the world, one country a time, is called the Holocaust. During the Holocaust, there were concentration camps all over Europe where Jewish people, Communists, and many others were imprisoned. Teachers were imprisoned just for protesting what Hitler and the Nazis were doing. Artists, musicians, and writers were deported to concentration camps if they opposed the Nazis, or expressed ideas that Hitler wanted to silence.

Living conditions in the concentration camps were unimaginably harsh. There was very little food and everyone starved on rations of watery soup. People lived crowded together in buildings called barracks—each with twenty to thirty bunk beds, and only one washroom. There was no heat in the cold of winter, and only flimsy clothes to wear. Often the inmates had to do forced labor to the point of exhaustion, in the worst of conditions. The guards beat the prisoners, and shot any who didn't follow orders exactly. There were no doctors, nor any medicine, to help people when they got sick. It was a huge struggle to survive from one day to the next. Many inmates went to the electrified fences around the camps and committed suicide to release themselves from the horror.

In late autumn 1942, Friedl and her husband received their deportation notices, and on December 14, 1942, were sent to Terezin, a concentration camp set up inside an old fortress close to the city of Prague. Of all of the concentration camps that existed during the Holocaust, Terezin was unique. The Nazis decided to put creative people whose work they had outlawed into one camp, and that place was Terezin. It would be a "showcase" so the Nazis could prove to the rest of the world that their prisoners were treated well, that inmates played music, painted, and put on plays. Imprisoned there

NAZI DEPORTATION

Getting a deportation order was a fearful event. You would arrive home one day from work or school, and waiting for you would be a document called a deportation notice. On that notice would be your name, and where you were ordered to report for your deportation. Few escaped deportation, because police were always watching. Usually, deportees had to report to a train station and were allowed to take only one suitcase. There, everyone was packed into hot, crowded cattle cars, on trains that normally carried livestock, not people. These trains carried the deportees to Nazi concentration camps, where they became prisoners.

were musicians, writers, painters, and other kinds of artists. Along with the artists, there were also a great many children. Most of them had been separated from their mothers and fathers, who were prisoners in other camps far away—or, worse, who had already died at the hands of the Nazis.

You would think that even in slightly less desperate conditions, the prisoners at Terezin would have lost any will to live. But an atmosphere of creativity and artistic expression set Terezin apart from the other concentration camps. Inside the camp, the adult musicians, writers and painters worked alone and in groups to create art that expressed their experiences and feelings and gave them some comfort. The artists of Terezin decided to use their special talents to help the children in the camp. Many of the artists, including Friedl, became teachers, to help the children through these darkest of days.

Operating a real school in Terezin was against the camp rules, and the Nazis only allowed the children to do simple crafts, such as sewing or making pretty greeting cards as decorations. But Friedl and other art teachers taught the children in secret. During her art classes, one of the children always acted as a lookout outside the door. Whenever it looked as if a Nazi camp guard was walking in their direction, the lookout would give a signal. The students would quickly hide their drawings and pencils, then sing and pretend to clean the room, so that the guard would not suspect anything.

In her art lessons, Friedl focused on showing the kids how to draw and paint. She taught them how to draw basic shapes, then to create textures and color combinations, encouraging them to create pictures of things that they missed. As you might expect, the kids drew bright flowers, their furry pets, or the homes where they had lived before becoming prisoners. Friedl believed that encouraging the children to draw beautiful pictures of their past lives would give them a welcome escape from the hard reality of the concentration camp.

Some of the art produced by children in the camp depicted happy days and peaceful everyday scenes like the ones above. They were drawn by Hana Brady, one of Friedl Dicker-Brandeis' students.

Some of their art was very beautiful. Kids drew landscapes with wide, green fields, rainbows, and gorgeous sunsets. Friedl wondered how they could create such extraordinary pictures from their imaginations. Were these memories from their past lives? When she asked the students to describe their pictures, she saw that they meant something different from what she had thought. The children told her they were drawing pictures of the world that they wanted to live in some day. For them, their art represented what they wished for when they could leave this prison behind.

Friedl's students were creating another kind of art that she knew had to be kept even more secret from the Nazi prison guards. The children of Terezin were making pictures that showed exactly what they were experiencing at the camp, and how they felt about it. For example, at Terezin, as in other concentration camps, many prisoners perished of hunger or illness, or were murdered by the guards. The children actually saw these horrific events unfold before their own eyes, and then described them in their art. Every day, Friedl's young students showed her pictures of people being shot, or pictures of those who had already died being taken away by the guards.

There was a third kind of art that their teacher found especially disturbing. Friedl showed her students how to make self-portraits. The young artists looked at themselves in mirrors and then drew or painted pictures of what they saw. The results really didn't surprise her, though they upset her very much. The children created self-portraits that pictured themselves as they really looked—skinny, underfed, and terrified.

Friedl realized that the artwork created by her students were not just pictures, but reflections of their hopes, dreams, nightmares, and real lives. She knew that the Nazi guards must never find these pictures. If the guards saw this artwork, it would be destroyed, and they would immediately punish or even kill the children who had created them. Instinctively, she also realized that the art of the children of Terezin had to be kept safe for another important reason. Whether the prisoners at Terezin survived or not, their art would be proof of their existence and suffering. And it would live on after them. So, once each picture was finished, Friedl had her student sign and date it. Then, she hid it with the rest in a cardboard box or in her suitcase, to ensure that the guards wouldn't see it.

In the evenings, she would discuss the pictures with teachers who knew about new ways of using art to help children and adults deal with their feelings. Friedl wanted to understand the drawings more deeply, so that she could give the children emotional support. She asked one boy, for instance, to write a poem to go along with his especially sad picture. Here's what he wrote:

Ah, home, home,
Why did they tear me away?
Here the weak die as easy as a feather
And when they die, they die forever.

The child who created this art and wrote this poem needed help to deal with his painful feelings. So, even though she wasn't trained for that job, Friedl became an art therapist for her students. She would ask them to explain what was in their pictures, and how they felt about it. Then she would do the best she could to give the children some comfort.

Friedl continued her work with the children for almost two years. All the while, she also painted and drew works of great beauty. However, in the fall of 1944, the event that everyone in Terezin feared the most finally took place. Hitler and the Nazis were beginning to lose their war against the Allied armies, and Hitler didn't want to leave the people he despised alive, or to leave witnesses to his barbaric crimes against humanity. The

"Final Solution" was his plan to transport any remaining prisoners to death camps, where they would be murdered in huge numbers. On September 28, 1944, Pavel was deported from Terezin to a death camp called Auschwitz. On October 6, Friedl volunteered to be on the next transport train to Auschwitz, so that she could be with her husband.

Friedl did reach Auschwitz, but just three days after she arrived, she was killed in a neighboring death camp called Birkenau along with about fifty of her students. Pavel managed to survive at Auschwitz. To make the tragedy even worse, the war against the Nazis ended in May 1945, only a few months after Friedl's death.

When the war was over, soldiers from the Russian army marched into Terezin to free the prisoners who were still alive. Miraculously, one of Friedl's students, a teenage girl named Raja, found more than five thousand of the children's drawings in suitcases that Friedl had hidden in the barracks. There were some of Friedl's own paintings there, too. Raja gave the artwork to a teacher named Willi Groag, who took it all to Prague. This important art sat boxed on a shelf in Prague for ten years before it was discovered and shown to the world.

Today, the art of the children of Terezin is displayed internationally. It belongs to the State Jewish Museum in Prague and another museum called Beit Theresienstadt (Terezin) in Israel. Two years after Friedl died, in 1947, the Czech government established the Terezin Memorial Museum on the spot where the prison had been. In the museum are one or two pieces of Friedl's own art, and some of the drawings done by the students she'd lovingly encouraged and inspired.

Friedl Dicker-Brandeis never imagined that she would become an influential teacher. If she had lived in another time, many art experts agree that her talents would have brought her fame as one of the great artists of the 20th century. But Friedl's legacy, her gift to the world, went far beyond that. This extraordinary woman never had children of her own, but she was a mother to hundreds of lonely, suffering kids. To these concentration camp children, living in the most horrifying conditions, she passed on her love of art and her understanding of the human soul. Friedl was able to use her gifts to nurture young artists so that they could describe their lives and dreams. Many of her students did not survive the Holocaust, but the stories told in their art remain with us forever.

MARVA COLLINS

Every
Kid
Counts

1936 -

When the rock star, Prince, visited Chicago's Westside Preparatory School in the middle of a concert tour, what he saw brought tears to his eyes. In fact, Prince was so impressed that he donated millions of dollars to make sure that the school's doors would stay open. He said, "This is the kind of school that I've always wanted to go to."

This very special school was created by a teacher named Marva Collins. She has changed the lives of thousands of students that others had given up on. Her own words give insight into how she managed to achieve what she did: "What everybody says can't be done becomes a challenge to me. My attitude has always been that I can do anything anyone else has done. It's a matter of the choices that I make." Marva's dedication to educating kids that others found to be unteachable has made her one of the most famous teachers in the United States.

Marva Collins was born Marva Deloise Nettles on August 31, 1936, in the state of Alabama. When Marva was growing up, segregation was a way of life that unfairly separated African Americans in the South from their neighbors, in almost every aspect of daily life. African Americans did not have equal rights with whites. Black people were not allowed to use the public library or many other public facilities, and black children had to attend separate, segregated schools. Often, these segregated schools were ill-equipped, and didn't have proper teaching materials with the most up-to-date information. Students had to make do with old books and poor learning conditions that were far worse than what was available for white children.

For a black child in the South like Marva, getting a decent education was no easy matter, but from a very young age, she wanted to learn. Marva had a family who loved her and supported her ambitions. In fact, her childhood was wonderful. Her father, Alex Nettles, was very important in her life. He had several careers, including being a successful businessman. Although he was always busy, working hard to support his family, her father took time to pay special attention to Marva and her younger sister Cynthia, and interested himself in their education.

When she was still a young child, Marva's father gave her serious jobs to do, which helped to build her confidence and sense of responsibility. For example, her father asked her to arrange the shelves in his store, to keep track of the bills, and to deposit the store's money in the bank. He never gave her "baby work." Instead, he entrusted her with essential jobs that were needed to run his business, and kept his daughter motivated to do her best work. Marva realized that she felt great when she was able to set herself a high goal and then meet it. Later, when she became a teacher, she always remembered to give that same feeling to her own students.

After she graduated from high school, Marva attended Clark College in Atlanta, Georgia. She wanted to become a secretary (an office assistant who takes dictation and types business letters, answers the phone, organizes her boss's schedule, and does the filing).

After earning her college degree in secretarial sciences in 1957, Marva returned to Alabama to teach typing (which we now call keyboarding) and other business subjects, at Monroe County Training School. But Marva had always thought that she would use her skills as a secretary to work in an office. After some time she left teaching to become a medical secretary in a Chicago hospital—a good job, even though it took her far from home. While she was working there, she met and married Clarence Collins. In 1961, Marva realized how much she missed working with students and helping them to discover the joy of learning. She decided that she wanted to help children

CAREER CHOICES

In the 1950s, women like Marva didn't have the same career choices that are available now. Many young women studied to work in junior office positions. Along with teaching and nursing, being a secretary was considered one of the few acceptable careers for a woman. Until the late 1960s, very few high schools, colleges, or universities encouraged women to study to be doctors, lawyers, engineers, or accountants, or to enter any other profession. Even if a woman did finish college or university in those days, she was often expected to get married and have children right away. And it was difficult for women to pursue a career once they had families to take care of, since society disapproved.

develop the self-respect, pride, and independence that had been instilled in her by her own father. Marva chose to devote herself to becoming the best teacher she could be. She studied teaching at the Chicago Teachers College and Columbia University. For fourteen years, she worked as a substitute teacher in the public schools of Chicago, taking over from regular classroom teachers, when the regular teachers had to be away from school. Substitute teachers have a challenging job. They walk into a brand new classroom almost every day and are expected to teach just as well as the regular classroom teacher. Marva's self-confidence and intelligence helped her to quickly adapt to and teach new groups of kids all the time.

Marva loved working as a substitute teacher. During those fourteen years, getting to know and work with so many different children, Marva gained a lot of experience with teaching bright students, and equally loved helping those who struggled in school. But this dedicated teacher was also disappointed by some things that she saw in these classrooms.

She could see that many of the kids she was teaching were reading two or three grades below their grade level, and it was obvious that they needed a lot of individual attention to catch up. But instead of getting extra help, these students were being given easier reading, or puzzles that would keep them busy. Marva believed that in most cases the children were not being challenged to do their best.

Why weren't these kids getting the extra help and encouragement that they needed? In Marva's opinion, there were quite a few reasons. First of all, there were the absences. Some children lived in very poor neighborhoods with high crime rates. So, students who were frustrated with their schoolwork often got distracted by whatever was happening on the streets, which they found much more exciting than sitting in class. These kids skipped many days of school, yet they were the ones who could least afford to miss classes. Some dropped out completely. She worried about their future.By this time, Marva was a mother. She knew that most parents deeply love and care about their children. But some of her students' parents had to work long hours to make enough money to support their families. Sometimes such hardworking parents weren't able to spend time helping their kids with homework, or visiting the school to talk with the teachers. Marva remembered how important her father's involvement was when it came to her own education, how he had inspired her to do her best. These children were not getting that encouragement.

Marva also saw that the schools themselves created problems. For one thing, the classes were usually far too big. Students who needed extra help weren't getting much. Their teachers had to help too many, and they had to deal with kids acting up in the crowded classrooms as well. Children who had a hard time understanding their schoolwork often got left behind. To make matters worse, their classmates would tease them and call them names. Finally, after observing the situation for nearly fifteen years, Marva realized that many teachers in Chicago's public school system had become frustrated and discouraged. They spent most of their time managing their overcrowded classrooms. Dealing with behavior problems was their number one activity—they didn't have the time or energy to teach their classes well. The saddest part of this situation was that the kids who needed the most help seemed to just give up. Many students became dropouts—or did barely enough work to graduate, but with very low marks. According to Marva, what was the point of scraping by, barely passing with a D average, if you couldn't get into college or even apply for a good job?

Marva's own two children attended expensive private schools in Chicago. One day, to her complete surprise, her kids confessed that they were as bored as the public school students she was teaching. A light went on in Marva's mind. She realized that the quality of a child's education didn't depend on how much money the school had, but on other things altogether. Marva decided that it was time to make a difference. She retired from being a public school teacher to start her own school.

In 1975, with only $5,000, Marva Collins opened the Westside Preparatory School. She didn't have a regular school building, and taught out of her own home. She started with about twenty students, from the ages of four to fourteen. In fact, the first class at Westside Preparatory School also included Marva's own children. Some of Westside Prep's new students had been expelled or rejected by school after school: most of them had been classified as unteachable. They were very weak in reading, writing, math and other subjects, and many had serious behavior problems. In the beginning, Marva kept her school small, to give each child a great deal of individual time and attention. She also demonstrated her independent attitude when it came to accepting help for her school. Marva could have easily applied for money from the government to help her financially with Westside Prep. But then she would have had to run the school according to their rules and regulations, and Marva had strong feelings about this. The public school system hadn't helped these children succeed, so why should she take their money? At Westside Prep, expectations for students' progress were going to be much higher than they had been in their public schools. The government wasn't going to tell her how to teach her students.

Marva Collins had her own specific ideas about teaching, and not every teacher or student would agree with or appreciate them. But her methods got the outstanding results she was aiming for. Each morning at her school, students began the day by reciting a poem that celebrated the choice to think positively, be responsible, and achieve goals. "We greet two hundred children every day, and each one tells us their plan

Marva Collins with students at her
inner-city Westside Preparatory School

for the day. They come to lunch and bring a topic they're going to discuss," Marva said, explaining her system.

After the poetry reading, students worked for four hours straight without a break. No recess. Students and teachers got only a half hour for lunch, and then it was back to work for another three hours. At the end of the school day, students who needed extra help were offered up to two hours of additional tutoring from their teachers. This was certainly a demanding schedule—and that is how the staff and students at Westside Prep spent every day.

Students at Westside Preparatory wore uniforms, and their classrooms were quiet, orderly places. You certainly wouldn't have found any cell phones there. There were no gym classes or after-school sports: students spent all their time improving their reading, math, and language skills. In this school, no student ever said, "I'm done with my work." When a teacher was satisfied that a student had finished an assignment well enough, that student quietly read a book for the rest of the class time. They had to be real books, not comic books, and everyone was challenged to read a longer book than they had read the time before. Just as Marva's father didn't give her "baby work" when she was a child, Marva wanted students to have new challenges, and to see that they could succeed

HELP WANTED
Teachers at Westside Prep gave students a lot of individual attention. Each teacher walked up and down the rows of the classroom, closely examining each student's work. If they wanted help, their teacher was right there, ready to give them a hand at their desk. This highly structured type of school may not be right for everyone, but Marva Collins believed that this is what her students needed, in order to do their best.

even if something seemed hard at first. Marva Collins believed that a traditional kind of classroom is the best place to learn, and for this reason some might think that she was very "old school." For example, the children all sat in rows of desks. There was no group learning, or learning through the class sharing experiences. Instead, the teacher was responsible for presenting all of the work to the students—it was her job to stimulate the kids and get them thinking.

Marva's main goal was to teach her students to think for themselves. She believed this is the most important skill in the long run. After all, if you can think through the answer to one tough question, you can use the same skill to solve many kinds of problems, big and small. Marva Collins didn't permit her teachers to use the workbooks or worksheets that many teachers used in their classes every day. To her, filling in the blanks was just not challenging enough. Her students focused on assignments that taught them to think independently. Every day after the kids finished reading, they wrote letters to the characters in their books, or to the authors. They wrote reviews in which they gave their opinions about what they'd read. They answered questions that really got them thinking. "Which character do I identify with the most? Why? What does this character teach me? What life lesson can I learn from reading this story?"

The success of Marva's students made her extremely proud. It is an extraordinary achievement that all of the graduates of Westside Prep—some of whom could barely sit still in class before they began, let alone read—have gone on to college. "Our students are self-motivated, self-generating and self-propelled," she once decared.

Marva Collins has become very well known because of her ideas about education and due to the success of her students. A newspaper article about her and the school appeared only two years after Westside Prep opened. Then, her story

Independent and strong-willed, Marva Collins had no time for failure. Her students were expected to succeed.

was broadcast on the CBS News program *60 Minutes,* and she became known to millions. In 1981, there was even a TV movie made, *The Marva Collins Story.* Over the years she has been profiled in many newspaper and magazine articles, and Marva has written several books to explain her teaching methods. Famous people, including the rock star Prince, have donated money to support Marva's National Teacher Training Institute, where she prepares teachers who want to use her methods in their classrooms. Marva has received numerous awards and honors, and has given speeches to more than 100,000 educators and business people. There are now five schools in the United States that use her methods exclusively.

After Marva left Westside Prep to continue writing books and spreading the word, the staff of her school included her daughter Cynthia, who, at the age of five, had been one of the school's original twenty students. Cynthia later became Westside's principal. Marva's son Patrick is active in teaching teachers and school administrators all over the United States about her methods.

One of Westside Prep's most famous students was college basketball star Kevin Ross. When he had graduated from college, and was already in his twenties, Kevin decided to enroll at Westside. Even though he'd finished college, he knew that he'd skated by on his athletic talents. He couldn't read, write, or do math well enough to get along in the real world. Within one school year, Kevin was able to improve all of his math and language skills dramatically. Marva asked Kevin to speak at a Grade 8 graduation ceremony, and his words showed that he took in more than reading and math from his teacher:

"Learn, learn, and learn some more. That way, no one will ever be able to say that inner-city children have no potential and no hope. You and I know that those people are wrong."

In 2008, Westside Prep had to close because of a bad economy in the U.S. Marva had never taken endowments from the government, so not many students could afford the tuition. The school went online, where it is now accessible to many more.

Marva Collins has spent her life transforming her students' lives, bringing them from failure to success. By her own example, she has demonstrated that hard work and tenacity really do pay off. This teacher has proved something very important. She maintains that no matter what other people think you can or cannot do, it's really up to you to achieve the goals you set for yourself. Marva knows you can do it.

CHRISTA McAULIFFE

A Fearless Heart

1948 - 1986

Christa McAuliffe, the first teacher ever to travel to space, achieved worldwide fame for her contribution to the American space program. But her story is forever connected to a spectacular tragedy.

Christa McAuliffe was born Sharon Christa Corrigan on September 2, 1948 in Boston, Massachusetts. She was raised, along with her four brothers and sisters, in the small community of Framingham, Massachusetts. Her father was an accountant, and her mother was a substitute teacher. The oldest child in the family, she was by nature responsible and mature—someone who always really enjoyed helping others. She enthusiastically joined the Brownies and later the Girl

Scouts of America, clubs that encourage girls to be self-reliant and community-minded. Christa was athletic and pursued quite a few interests and hobbies. She loved to be outdoors as much as possible, and spent her summers at a camp in New Hampshire. Skiing and softball were her favorite sports, and music also played an important part in her life. While she was in high school, she studied the piano, and had fun performing in all the school musicals.

Like many kids who grew up in the 1960s, Christa was fascinated by a big international event of the time—The Space Race. The race to explore space was fueled by intense competition between the United States and the Soviet Union (today called Russia). These two world powers had begun exploring space in 1957, when they started to send up unmanned rockets. These were followed by rockets carrying animals into space (a Russian dog named Laika was the first animal to go up), and, finally, by capsules that carried astronauts into space. The competition was about which country would reach certain milestones first—who would be the first to send a rocket into space, the first to orbit the Earth, the first to send up a woman astronaut? People everywhere followed the Space Race avidly.Throughout her teen years, Christa, too, read up on and followed all these sensational space events, which were shown live on television to the amazement of millions around the world.

Christa was especially inspired by the brave American pilot John Glenn, who was the first astronaut from any country to orbit the Earth. His spacecraft was called *Friendship 7.* The day after she witnessed his historic journey on TV, Christa exclaimed to her classmate, "Do you realize that some day people will be going to the Moon? Maybe even taking a bus, and I want to do that."

After high school, Christa went to Framingham State College right in her hometown, graduating in 1970 with a degree in education and history. A few weeks after graduation, she married Steven McAuliffe, her boyfriend since high school, and they moved close to Washington, D.C., so that Steven could study to be a lawyer.

Christa spent the next few years becoming an outstanding and unforgettable teacher. She taught American history in a junior high school, and then history and civics in middle school. Because Christa had a real thirst for knowledge and was always striving to become an even better teacher, she went back to university and completed a Master's degree in Education. She also became a mother, and had two children, Scott and Caroline.

Christa was always keenly aware that the world was changing fast. Since Christa taught social studies, history, law, and economics, it was very important to her that her students have the most up-to-date picture of what was happening in the real world outside the classroom. At that time, the Internet wasn't available to help her and her students research the latest ideas. Instead, she brought in exciting experts to talk to the class, and often took her students on field trips that brought the ideas in their textbooks to life. She explored the part that women played in American history, and created her own course called "The American Woman" for her students. *The New York Times* heard about her outstanding classes, and praised Christa's teaching, reporting that she "emphasized the impact of ordinary people on history, saying that they're as important to the historical record as kings, politicians or generals." In focusing on the way that ordinary people contribute to history, Christa was unknowingly predicting something about her own story.

In 1984, then-U.S. President Ronald Reagan announced the creation of a Teacher in Space Program. This program would be run by NASA, the National Aeronautics and Space Administration, the same organization that had trained the astronauts who had fascinated the young Christa, and sent them into space. Now NASA was looking for a teacher to be the first civilian to travel aboard the Space Shuttle.

Up to then, all the astronauts had been army or air force officers. Some had even been test pilots, flying airplanes so fast that they broke the sound barrier. Other astronauts were pilots who had also earned degrees in science, engineering, or medicine. They conducted complex experiments during their space missions to help add new knowledge to space science. However, this time NASA recruiters weren't looking for a pilot or a scientist; they were looking for a teacher, someone who could communicate well to students all over the world. In fact, the teacher they chose would teach directly from the spacecraft. NASA planned to broadcast the lesson by satellite, so that it could be watched on TV by millions of adults and children back on Earth.

Both NASA and President Reagan had special reasons for wanting teachers to participate in the space program. During the 1960s when Christa was growing up, everyone was so excited by space travel that they would stay glued to their televisions for hours, watching rockets take off into space and astronauts walk on the moon. However, by the early 1980s, when Christa was teaching her classes near Washington, the American people seemed far less interested in space travel. Maybe it was because they'd gotten used to seeing astronauts travel to space. Added to this, there was a growing awareness of the dangers of space travel. Americans had watched on TV as astronauts had barely escaped death. One mission to the moon, *Apollo 13*, had such severe technical problems that the astronauts almost didn't make it back to Earth. Both American and Soviet astronauts had actually died in spacecraft accidents and rocket explosions. It seemed that few still shared Christa's sense of adventure about exploring space, and it was getting harder for the American government to justify continuing with its very expensive space program. President Reagan thought that having a teacher participate in a space flight would get young people and adults excited about space exploration again.

Once the Teacher in Space project was announced, more than 11,000 men and women applied for the job. Christa was one of them. Here is a bit of what she wrote in her application: "I cannot join the space program and restart my life as an astronaut, but this opportunity to connect my abilities as an educator with my interests in history and space is a unique opportunity to fulfill my early fantasies." It's clear from Christa's words that traveling to space was a dream that she had held in her heart since she was a child. Her application showed quiet confidence that her passion for space exploration, and her skills as a teacher, would make her just the right person for the job.

NASA officials carefully sifted through and read the huge piles of applications for the position of first teacher in space. On July 1, 1985, almost a year after the plan had been announced, Christa was selected as one of the ten finalists. A few days later, she traveled to the Johnson Space Center in Florida to undergo tough medical tests to make sure that she was strong enough to fly to space. She and the other nine finalists also had information sessions about life on board the space shuttle, so that they would have an idea of what to expect if they were chosen.

A panel of former astronauts, NASA officials, teachers, and professional athletes interviewed each of the ten finalists. When asked why she wanted to be chosen for this special honor, Christa said, "I've always been concerned that ordinary people have not been given their place in history. I would like to humanize the space age by giving the perspective of a non-astronaut. Space is the future. As teachers, we prepare the students for the future. We have to include it. Space is for everyone." During her interview, Christa also said that she wanted to keep a diary with every detail of her adventure in space, so that she could share it after landing.

Obviously the special panel liked what she had to say. On July 19, 1985, NASA made the formal announcement that Christa McAuliffe would be the first teacher in space. In September, she started an intensive four-month training program to prepare for her journey. She attended many briefings about how the space shuttle worked, and learned about the experiments that would be done aboard the mission. She learned to read scientific and computer data from the state-of-the-art equipment used on the shuttle. She practiced launch and landing procedures with the rest of the crew, and learned how to operate the onboard cameras. Christa also memorized how to operate the controls and carry out emergency procedures. She trained to withstand massive "G-force," a sudden surge of gravity's force on your body at lift off.

Christa became a media star during her astronaut training, and appeared on many TV shows. Her talkative, bubbly personality made her the perfect guest, and a superb spokesperson. People were just drawn to her. It looked as if the idea of putting a teacher in space was really working. Christa McAuliffe's involvement was breathing new life into the space program, making it popular again with children and adults everywhere.

But it would be a mistake to think that Christa's participation was just a publicity stunt. She had very important responsibilities aboard the mission. Her planned duties included performing science experiments with magnets, and others to prove Newton's Laws of Gravity. And of course, she was also preparing two fifteen-minute classes to teach from space. One was titled "The Ultimate Field Trip," and would give viewers a detailed tour of the spacecraft. The second, "Where We've Been, Where We're Going, and Why," would show how

FLOATING IN SPACE

One of the most challenging things Christa learned was how to perform her assigned tasks while weightless. She joined the astronauts on the "Vomit Comet." This fixed-wing aircraft flies high above the Earth, then makes a steep curving dive that removes gravity for 30-second training periods. In near-zero gravity, the astronauts float, and experience what it is like to work, move around, and even eat while weightless in space. (The nickname of the plane tells us what a first reaction might be).

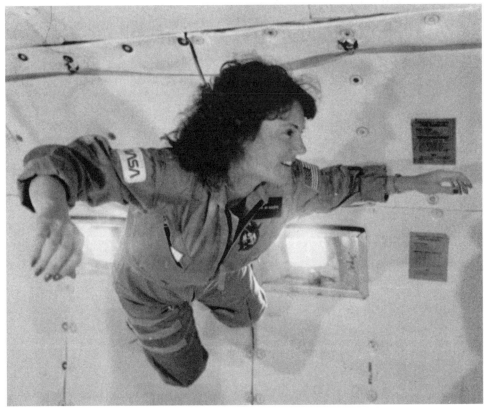

It might look like fun, but Christa and the others found it a challenge to learn how to carry out their duties while weightless.

discoveries in space have helped people in the past, and would continue to do so in the future.

Excitement grew as the launch of the Space Shuttle *Challenger* approached. On January 28, 1986, Christa McAuliffe and the six other astronauts donned their gear and boarded the spacecraft, as millions around the world watched on TV and cheered them on. The countdown and lift-off proceeded smoothly—but only 73 seconds into the flight, the unthinkable happened. As the spacecraft was climbing into the atmosphere, it exploded into flames at an altitude of 48,000 feet, and then the fiery wreckage plummeted into the Atlantic. All seven of the crewmembers died. Countless millions watched the successful liftoff on their TV screens and then stared, horrified, as this enormous tragedy unfolded before their eyes.

Christa's family laid her to rest in Blossom Hill Cemetery, near her home in Concord, New Hampshire. The legacy of her

The *Challenger* team posed proudly for photographers before their mission. All seven perished when the shuttle exploded.

accomplishment and sacrifice has been honored in many ways. The Christa McAuliffe Planetarium in Concord, Massachusetts and the Christa Corrigan McAuliffe Center for Education and Teaching Excellence at Framingham State College are both named in her memory. Scientists have even recognized Christa by naming an asteroid, a moon crater, and a crater on the planet Venus after her. The honor that probably would have touched Christa the most is that since her death, about forty schools all over the world have been named after her.

Scholarships and educational events have been created in her memory. Every year since 1986, The Christa McAuliffe Technology Conference, which explores the best ways to use technology in education, has been held in her home state of New Hampshire. Also, in Christa's memory, The American Association of State Colleges and Universities and the National Council for the Social Studies have given financial grants in her honor to teachers who use new and fresh ideas to inspire their students.

Films, television, and music have also done their part in keeping Christa's memory alive. In 1990, the movie *Challenger* was made for television. A children's science-fiction series called *Space Cases*, about a group of classmates lost in space, featured a spacecraft named the *Christa*. In 2006, CNN produced the documentary *Christa McAuliffe: Reach for the Stars* to mark the twentieth anniversary of her death, and Carly Simon wrote the title song.

You might be curious to know what happened to Christa's family. Christa's parents worked with the Framingham State College to establish the McAuliffe Center for Education in her honor. Her husband Steven did marry again, and became a judge in New Hampshire. Both of Christa's children, who are now adults, have followed in her footsteps, but in different ways. Her son, Scott, inherited his mother's adventurous spirit and is a marine biologist studying the science of sea life.

Caroline has become a teacher. On July 23, 2004, Christa was posthumously awarded the Congressional Space Medal of Honor by President George W. Bush, in recognition of her sacrifice and the contribution she would have made if she had still been with us.

It is difficult to measure Christa McAuliffe's legacy, because her life was cut so short. We will never know about all of the wonderful lessons that she could have taught. However, some have continued what Christa had begun. One such person is Barbara Morgan. Barbara was Christa's "back-up," a teacher who had been chosen by NASA at the same time as Christa, and who trained along with her. Barbara would have replaced Christa on the mission if Christa got sick or couldn't go for some other reason. Obviously Barbara didn't go on *Challenger*. However, she did carry on Christa's work. She became a professional astronaut in January 1998 and in 2007 flew on a mission to the International Space Station on the space shuttle *Endeavour*, the one that replaced *Challenger*. In accomplishing that goal, Barbara Morgan became the first teacher to successfully reach space, twenty-one years after Christa's death. Through her courage and spirit of adventure, Christa motivated another teacher to take the long road into space and become an astronaut herself. Perhaps this was Christa's greatest gift: inspiring others to do exceptional things.

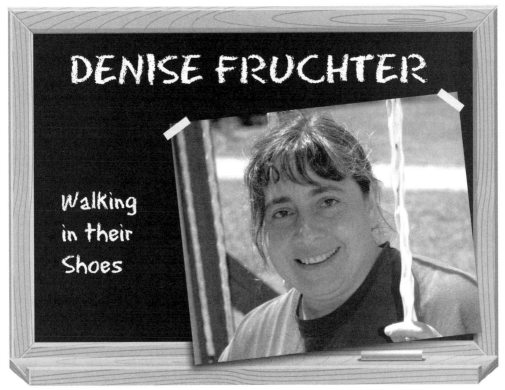

DENISE FRUCHTER

Walking
in their
Shoes

1956 –

Have you ever thought about the personal qualities you'd need to teach kids with special challenges? The first words to come to mind might be patience and understanding, but some teachers also possess a remarkable ability to get inside the hearts and minds of children with special needs. Denise Fruchter is one of these teachers. What makes Denise really exceptional is that she managed to finish high school and university and go on to a successful teaching career, all while dealing with her own disabilities—Tourette's Syndrome, ADHD, and other learning challenges.

Denise Fruchter has dedicated herself to making sure that special needs children can have experiences that most kids take for granted. As someone with special needs herself, she realizes how difficult it is for these kids to feel like they fit in with others. The unpredictable ways that their brains and bodies behave make this almost impossible. Their special challenges create walls between them and the friends they would like to make, and the activities that they dream of doing. Denise Fruchter is in a position to truly understand how much they really want to be like everyone else.

When we speak of children with special needs, we are usually thinking about kids with physical disabilities, who use crutches, wheelchairs, or walkers. People who are blind or deaf also need extra help in school, and with their daily activities.

Many students with physical disabilities can enjoy whatever activities they would like. Sometimes all they need is a little extra coaching or adapted equipment that helps them to play sports, dance, sing in a choir, or act in a play. They can choose to enjoy these activities in their own small classes, where their teachers can give them a lot of individual, extra help. But nowadays, more and more physically disabled kids are in regular classes and after-school clubs. Everyone wants

SCHOOL DAYS FOR ALL

In Canada, the United States, and Europe, schools, from daycare through to college and university, do their best to help students with physical disabilities participate in activities just like anyone else. Numerous schools have ramps and elevators so that kids with physical disabilities can easily get to any room in the building. Visually impaired students use materials with larger print for their schoolwork, and blind students are provided with Braille and audio books. Children who are hearing-impaired have hearing aids to assist them. Deaf children sometimes learn to read lips, or have sign language interpreters who help them achieve success at school.

kids with physical disabilities to have the chance to take part in school or extracurricular activities—just like the other kids. But there are some special needs kids who have a much harder time fitting in. These kids have difficulties connected to how their brains work. Tourette's Syndrome is one of these disabilities. Kids and adults who have Tourette's face great obstacles every day because their brains cause them to act strangely or to do things that the rest of us might regard as strange. People with Tourette's often have facial tics, which means that parts of their faces twitch repeatedly. Also, they sometimes make odd noises or even use swear words when they're trying to have a conversation. They cannot control any of these things.

People with Tourette's Syndrome are often misunderstood, and may make other people uncomfortable. Once you are aware that someone with Tourette's is struggling with a brain that acts on its own—sometimes in embarrassing ways—you can sympathize with what they're going through.

Try to imagine how you would feel if you had to deal with Tourette's every day. Most kids and adults don't know anything about this condition. They think that someone who acts this way must be doing it on purpose—swearing or making strange sounds or movements because they want to bother people or get attention. ADHD (Attention Deficit Hyperactivity

PUZZLING SYNDROME

Tourette's Syndrome is mysterious. Neurologists, who study the human brain, are working hard trying to figure out what causes it, and how to help people who have it. Some children with this condition can take medication that keeps it under control. But for less fortunate kids, having Tourette's is a nightmare. The sounds and movements that they make, yet cannot control, cause them to be shunned by other kids.

Disorder) is another condition that many children have to deal with. We've all seen students like this in our classes. They have a hard time sitting still, paying attention, and getting their work done on time. Sometimes the rest of us don't understand. Kids with ADHD are now helped by medications, and by learning ways to control their behavior. But often, they are still misunderstood by their classmates and teachers.

Autism is a range of conditions that some special needs students have. There is a milder type, called Asperger's Syndrome, where kids have problems socializing and communicating. Most children with Asperger's do well in after-school activities with the support of their teachers, family, and friends. But kids who have a more severe form of autism have a much harder time fitting in. You may have met autistic kids at school —often they need very small special needs classes because they can't communicate much or at all, and have difficulty controlling their tempers and feelings.

When they're at school, most children with brain disorders do feel helped and supported by dedicated teachers. Many are able to make some friends in their special needs classes, socialize with them at lunchtime, and play with them at recess. But what happens when these kids get home from school—who's around for them? Are there any other kids who understand what they're going through, understand their odd facial tics, behavior, and sounds, and who want to be their friends?

After teaching special education classes for children with Tourette's, ADHD, and autism for many years in Toronto, Denise decided to start a summer camp for kids facing these big challenges. She founded Camp Winston because she was able to walk in the shoes of the kids that she works with. She remembers what it was like being a ten-year-old who could not participate in social and recreational activities like everyone else she grew up with. From personal experience, Denise knows that these special needs kids, who don't look or act like "regular kids," have additional problems. For example, many kids with Tourette's, ADHD, or autism can't move or run very well, because they have poor co-ordination. These children may be eager to play sports and do other physical activities, but will never join in. Because they have a hard time communicating, they are easily embarrassed, too.

Denise knew all about these issues. She felt strongly that kids with brain disorders needed an enjoyable camp designed just for them, so that they could have fun, make friends, and learn new ways to cope. When she was growing up, Denise's parents sent her to a summer camp with regular kids. She tried hard to participate, but she just couldn't do it. Often she was asked to do things that were impossible for her, and she became ashamed. At the time, there weren't any summer programs for special needs kids, and Denise didn't have anyone who could help her. So, while the other kids at summer camp were playing baseball, riding horses, or swimming, Denise just ended up climbing a tree, waiting for everyone to finish. In the back of her mind she always thought there had to be a better way.

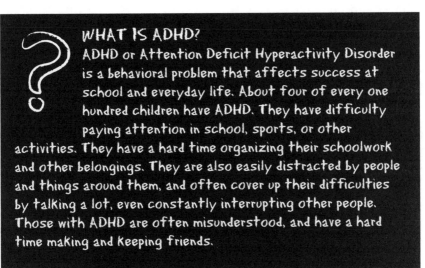

WHAT IS ADHD?

ADHD or Attention Deficit Hyperactivity Disorder is a behavioral problem that affects success at school and everyday life. About four of every one hundred children have ADHD. They have difficulty paying attention in school, sports, or other activities. They have a hard time organizing their schoolwork and other belongings. They are also easily distracted by people and things around them, and often cover up their difficulties by talking a lot, even constantly interrupting other people. Those with ADHD are often misunderstood, and have a hard time making and keeping friends.

In 1991, Denise opened her special needs summer camp. It's on a lake in the beautiful Canadian countryside of Muskoka, Ontario. For many kids with brain disorders, it's the first time that they have had the chance to go to camp, just like everybody else.

Many of the camp's counselors have brain disorders like the campers, and have a special connection with the kids. Because she's been through their experiences, Denise knows that the campers spend the rest of the year doing their best to fit in with everyone else. She understands, because she's "been there," that kids with brain disorders can feel left out and angry because they can't participate in fun activities that everyone else takes for granted. She also knows that these kids become lonely because there aren't many people who understand their feelings.

Since it began, Camp Winston has given numerous kids with special needs the wonderful summer camp experience that everyone deserves. Here are a few of their stories.

Christopher had already been expelled from sixteen summer camps for behavior such as starting fires and turning off the electricity. But after talking to him and to his parents, Denise accepted Christopher as a camper at Camp Winston, where he spent several very happy summers. He has since become a self-confident adult, and recently finished university. After college graduation, he decided to show his gratitude to Denise by becoming a camp counselor himself. Now he wants to help more young kids like him enjoy a great time at summer camp.

Dylan can't wait for school to end each year so that he can get to Camp Winston. What he loves about the camp are its special activities for kids with brain disorders. Dylan's favorite cabin is the one that all the kids call "Gross." It has special mats that look like giant building blocks, mini cars, and a pit full of balls. It's called Gross because the campers use it to improve their gross motor skills—the co-ordination of their big arm and leg muscles. Dylan, like many of the children who love to spend time in Gross, finds that moving around on blocks and balls and scooting around on wheels helps him to play and use up all of his energy, without getting hurt.

Denise and the counselors at Camp Winston have discovered that having all kinds of animals there has a wonderful effect on the campers. Some Camp Winston campers can hardly speak at all. If their parents were to put them in a camp with regular kids, how would they be able to make friends? Even though they can't speak, these campers have a lot of fun taking care of the animals in the nature shack. Holder, who is nine years old, loves helping to look after the turtles, a bunny, and a snake. Because they've been frightened by people who misunderstood them and called them names, kids with brain disorders who care for the animals learn to trust, and to give love to the animals—who love them in return, no matter what. Besides just having fun and learning to accept themselves, the children and teens at Camp Winston also work on their social skills. Because their neurological disorders cause them to behave in strange ways, they can be painfully shy and afraid to get to know other people. Although they make friends in their special education classes, they're often too shy and scared to find friends anywhere else. So, when they're not at school, kids with neurological disorders spend a lot of time by themselves.

Since she knows exactly how it feels to be so isolated, Denise has created a program at the camp that helps kids develop their social skills—all the ways that we learn to get along with each other. The rest of us learn these skills working on partner projects in school, being on sports teams, or participating in clubs or after school activities. But kids with neurological disorders miss out on most of these experiences. Denise knows that not having social skills can affect your whole life, so she has created many experiences that are very social at the camp.

Lorena was a teenager who never had fun at a regular camp. Being anxious a lot of the time, she always seemed to get into big fights with counselors and other kids. When she was fourteen years old, she became so nervous about going to class that her parents had to take her out of school. After she stopped going to school, Lorena's parents and doctors were afraid that she was becoming a hermit. She'd stay indoors by herself because she was too afraid of meeting and communicating with people. But at Camp Winston, she learned how to live peacefully in the cabin with other kids, to share, and to work problems out without getting angry or frustrated. Lorena really blossomed and started college. She has also returned to the camp as a counselor: now she's the one helping younger girls with their learning challenges. The kids at Camp Winston get all kinds of opportunities to overcome their fears and to understand teamwork—giant steps forward for anyone with a neurological disorder. One activity Denise created to help them is quite daring. The counselors carefully set up a rope bridge between two spruce trees, about 54 feet (18 metres) off the ground. Then, they challenge campers to climb up one of the trees and use the rope bridge to get to the other tree—either by walking on the rope, or by getting there hand over hand. However the campers choose to get across, they wear strong harnesses to keep them completely safe. Their counselors are below, helping to coach them across and cheering them on. This activity can be particularly helpful in building team skills when two campers cross together. In that case, they have to learn how to take turns and co-operate with each other so that both can get across safely. Imagine their sense of accomplishment when they overcome their fears and complete this amazing feat.

Campers who may not be quite ready for such risky

challenges practice their teamwork in other ways. When the kids at Camp Winston create art projects, they're also learning important skills such as how to accept criticism from a counselor or another camper, and how to comment on another person's work without hurting their feelings. Kids take care of an organic garden, where, working together, they grow fruits, vegetables, and herbs without any chemicals. There's also a theater center, where they can practice how to handle difficult situations through drama. For example, the counselors will help them to put on a play that shows kids working out a problem peacefully, instead of getting into a fight.

Instead of letting her brain disorders defeat her, Denise used her life experiences to create an extraordinary camp for kids who have felt just like she did. She's a living example of how we should never let our challenges overwhelm us. By creating and running Camp Winston, she's helping kids with these special needs become more comfortable in their own skins—to feel better about who they are and what they can accomplish. When it comes right down to it, isn't that what every kid wants and deserves?

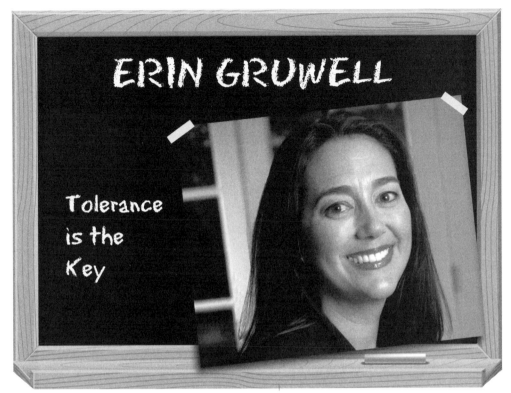

ERIN GRUWELL

Tolerance is the Key

1969 -

Few teachers become famous, but Erin Gruwell's Freedom Writers blog has become such an inspiration to teachers, students, and parents that it receives thousands of hits every day. Erin has also written a bestselling book, and she and her students have appeared on television, all before she turned thirty. Hollywood has even made a movie about her. At an age when most teachers are just establishing their careers, Erin Gruwell had already made a big impact on education with her exciting ideas and methods.

Erin was born in 1969 and grew up in California in a safe and comfortable suburb of Los Angeles. Her family was close, and her parents were very involved in her life. They encouraged her to do well in her studies, and she didn't disappoint them. Her goal had always been to be a teacher—the kind of teacher that every student remembers. She wanted to be the teacher who would open her students up to the wonderful world of language, and to the idea that loving words would open many doors to the possibilities in their lives.

Erin had her first taste of teaching in September 1994, when she was a new student teacher at Woodrow Wilson High School in Long Beach, California. Young, bright, and enthusiastic, she was optimistic about starting out in a new career, and eager to make an important contribution to her chosen profession. She especially loved writing, and was eager to pass on her love of words to her very first class of students.

But for a young woman who grew up in a safe neighborhood, she found herself in an unfamiliar situation. Long Beach can be a tough part of Los Angeles. Many people there are poor, and lots of kids have only one parent around as they're growing up. Erin's first class was full of students who had very poor marks, and some of them even had a history of violent behavior. Many kids grow up believing that their parents are there to love and protect them, so they have a natural trust of people in authority, like teachers or the police. But Erin's first class of students had led very different lives.

They were bitter and angry—tough kids who had never done well in school—and they had no respect for her or any teacher. These kids didn't see their parents much, sometimes because their parents were struggling financially, working two or three jobs. Sometimes there was only one parent at home, so there was extra pressure on that parent to pay the family bills and ensure that everyone had food, clothes, and all the other things the family needs. Often, through nobody's fault, these children were on their own a lot. When they got home from school their mothers or fathers weren't there waiting for them. The kids often made their own dinners and took care of household chores that their working parents hadn't had time to do, like doing laundry or taking care of their younger brothers and sisters.

Erin Gruwell's young students faced other challenges that any of us would find hard to cope with. As soon as she started teaching, Erin could see that some of her new students were victims of abuse. Someone at home was neglecting them, or was even mistreating them physically or emotionally. These kids were left alone for long periods of time without anyone they could call if there was an emergency. Often if there actually was a parent or older sibling at home, they might be violent due to drugs or alcohol.

The morning that Erin walked into her first class as a student teacher, dressed in her pink polka-dot dress, she faced a hostile group of teens. Quickly, it became clear to her that many of the students belonged to gangs. Kids who belong to gangs think of their gang as their new family: their real family has let them down, or abandoned them. As well as dressing alike and hanging out together, gang members do things to show their loyalty to each other. They might skip school to hang out in a group at the mall or a coffee shop. They'll stand around smoking, drinking, or bullying others. Because they're

DOMESTIC VIOLENCE

Being abused is a terrifying situation to deal with. Imagine if you lived with a parent or big brother or sister who repeatedly beat you whenever they thought you did something wrong, or if you didn't do exactly what they said. This is called physical abuse. Another kind of violence or abuse is when someone responsible for you constantly calls you bad names, yells at you, and makes you feel worthless and scared. This is emotional abuse. Many of Erin Gruwell's students coped with abuse every day.

angry with the world, they'll get into trouble by robbing people, or breaking into houses to steal things. Many gang kids have brushes with the law when they are as young as nine or ten, and continue to commit crimes when they become teenagers.

Gang members are often very violent. They believe that the only way to solve a problem or to get what they want is to fight for it, using a gun or knife if they have to. Unfortunately, even as early as elementary school, teachers and students can spot these kinds of kids in classrooms every day.

The eager new teacher saw that her students didn't trust her, and that they weren't interested in learning anything that she wanted to teach. Erin noticed right away that the kids sat in groups—either next to their friends who belonged to the same gangs, or with kids of the same color or nationality. They were so suspicious of one another that they never talked to each other, even during school hours. It was obvious to her that the gang wars in the neighborhood were also going on right there in her classroom. And although Erin was supposed to be teaching ninth grade, she quickly realized that most of her students were reading and writing several grades below their grade level.

Erin began by trying new ideas from her college textbooks to ease into teaching her tough students. Word games, puzzles, and other fun activities filled her classes, and she hoped these would strike a chord with her hard-to-reach kids. Some of the kids responded, but not many. One particular student seemed determined to make her life miserable by acting out constantly. In the book she wrote based on her experiences, Erin called this boy Sharaud. Sharaud had been transferred to Erin's school because he had threatened a teacher at his old school with a gun. She just could not get through to him. But a few months after the school year started, Erin caught one of the other students passing a really insulting picture of Sharaud's face around the class. The note showed Sharaud, who is African American, with cartoonishly large lips. His classmates were laughing at the picture. Sharaud felt humiliated. Even though he always gave her such a hard time, Erin's heart broke for him.

Erin became so disturbed by this incident that she set aside the course of study that she was supposed to teach. Instead, she decided to use her students' own behavior and attitudes as a way to reach them. She told her students that the picture making fun of Sharaud was an example of a stereotype. A stereotype, she explained, is an often insulting, description that exaggerates something about a person's looks or behavior or refers to their religious or ethnic group. Stereotypes are unjust and can be very destructive. There are lots of stereotypes that we can point to in our lives. Often, quiet, smart kids are cartooned wearing big, thick glasses, and are labeled nerds. Jewish people have been drawn with long, hooked noses and accused of plotting to take over the world. Another recent, totally unjust stereotype is that Muslims who wear their traditional clothing must be terrorists. When you are stereotyped like this, you feel insulted and scared that other people have really bad feelings about you.

Erin focused all of her lessons for the rest of the year on the theme of tolerance. She taught that instead of being afraid or suspicious of people who look or sound different from us, we need to understand those differences and treat people fairly. Erin introduced her students to movies and books that explored this idea. She took her students to see the movie *Schindler's List*, about one man who bravely stood against the Holocaust, a time in history when twelve million innocent men, women, and children, including six million Jews, were systematically murdered because of the stereotypes created by the Nazi dictator Adolf Hitler. For the rest of the school year, Erin spent her own money buying books that told stories of tolerance for her students. She also invited guest speakers to talk to the class about the ways stereotypes hurt, and toler-ance heals.

Erin returned to Woodrow Wilson High School the fol-lowing year, as a full teacher. Again, instead of following the curriculum she was supposed to teach, Erin did something new. She asked her students to make videos about their lives and to keep journals of their daily activities and emotions. They wrote about themselves to communicate their feelings, and to reach out to people who might understand them or help them to solve their problems. Sometimes, they wrote as a way to ease their loneliness and fears. Erin hoped that encouraging her students to write about themselves would help them in all of these ways, as well as make them more successful students. Erin told them not to put their names on their journals. Then, she had the kids trade journals, and read each other's writ-ings. Something miraculous happened.

Students who used to hate each other because they were from rival gangs or of different races, now began to under-stand and appreciate each other's lives. They began to treat each other as family members or friends, and not enemies. Instead of hanging on to their old gang names, the students created a new name for themselves: The Freedom Writers. They got the idea from reading the history of the Freedom Riders. These white men and women rode the buses with African American people in the South when they were being discriminated against, and forbidden to ride in the same part of the bus as whites.

Next, Erin tried something with her students that most would have thought impossible. She taught her students to read and understand *Romeo and Juliet*—the play by William Shakespeare that tells the love story of a boy and girl from two families who hate each other. Shakespeare wrote hundreds of years ago, and his language can be hard to understand, but Erin knew her students would connect with the story. She compared the feud between the two families in the play to the wars between fighting street gangs—which her students understood very well. They were swept away by the play and its language, too.

She also gave them books by teenagers who were living in times of war caused by intolerance. *Zlata's Diary* was written by a young girl living in the terrifying atmosphere of war-torn Sarajevo in the 1990s. *The Diary of Anne Frank,* one of the most famous books ever written, was the memoir of a thirteen-year-old Jewish girl hiding from the Nazis during World War II. Because they could see how important and powerful journal writing had been for these young people, Erin's students began to share even more of their thoughts and feelings in their own journals.

Erin gave each of her students a bag full of new books and had them make a promise to one another to continue to change their lives and attitudes. And in time The Freedom Writers—150 street kids that most teachers and administrators had given up on—all graduated from high school. Many of them went on to college.

In the next few years, Erin's successful teaching methods with the Freedom Writers program became famous. Stories about her classes often appeared on TV shows such as *Oprah, The View,* and *Good Morning America.* Erin decided that her students' journal writings were so important that they needed to be shared with a bigger audience. When the book, *The Freedom Writers Diary,* was published in 1999, it became a bestseller. It contained the journals of Erin's students, as well as descriptions of their lives, written in Erin's own words. In 2007, a film, called *Freedom Writers,* was released, with actress Hilary Swank playing Erin.

Erin Gruwell has gone on to even more accomplishments. After the publication of *The Freedom Writers Diary,* Erin felt that she could make a bigger contribution to education. She strongly believes that teaching tolerance is the key to encouraging students to stay in school and look to the future. So, after teaching at Woodrow Wilson High School for a few years, Erin created the Freedom Writers Foundation. Erin, and some of her successful Freedom Writers graduates, travel around the United States as motivational speakers. They talk to teachers and other groups of people who care about improving education. Erin shares her experiences in getting through to her hostile students. Many of the Freedom Writers, now college students and professional people, speak along with her, or give their own speeches about how they transformed their lives. She runs seminars and workshops for new teachers, giving them ideas for inspiring difficult students.

Then, in 2000, when she was just thirty years old, Erin decided that she wanted to become a member of Congress in the United States government, and ran for election. Although she did not win that election, she still travels the country with her message of hope, encouraging teachers and students to focus on the best and not the worst in themselves.

It's easy for teachers in big city schools to feel overwhelmed and sometimes discouraged by all of their challenges. Many of the students who walk into their classes seem to be almost impossible to reach. Although they're just kids, these students have been so hurt and disappointed in their short lives that they simply block out whatever is going on in the classroom. But Erin Gruwell has proven that it's the responsibility of every teacher not to give up. Teachers of challenging kids must do whatever they can to break through the walls of anger and resistance that these students put up. Her actions show us that instead of teaching what one is expected to teach, sometimes a teacher just needs to listen to her heart. For Erin Gruwell, teaching tolerance became the window that opened up the world to her students.

MALALAI JOYA

The Bravest Woman in Afghanistan

1978 -

Malalai Joya has been called the bravest woman in Afghanistan. Many people think that that she just might be the bravest woman anywhere. *TIME* magazine named her one of the 100 most influential people in the world for the year 2010. Malalai became famous for fighting to improve the rights of women in her native country. Risking her life on many occasions, she has dared to demand that girls in Afghanistan should have the same opportunities to get an education as boys, so that they'll have a chance for independence and a good future.

When she was only twenty-five years old, Malalai Joya became the youngest person ever to be elected to the new democratic government in Afghanistan. Although her life is in constant danger, this courageous young woman continues to speak out against the powerful men in her country who don't want girls and women to have the same opportunities as their brothers, husbands, and fathers.

Malalai was born on April 25, 1978, the oldest daughter in a big family, which includes her seven sisters and three brothers. When she was only four days old, a country called the Soviet Union, now known as Russia, invaded Afghanistan. Often when one country invades another, the local citizens are treated unjustly. The people of an invaded or occupied nation often can't even get the basic necessities such as food, clothing, and a safe place to live. They are frequently forced to leave their homes because the invading army takes over their houses for its own soldiers.

Malalai's father was studying to be a doctor when the Soviets invaded his country. He decided to join the rebel army, which was fighting against the invasion. Sadly, Malalai's father was wounded in battle, and lost one of his legs. Since her father couldn't continue fighting, the whole family left Afghanistan

LOSING YOUR HOMELAND

Unfortunately, many children and adults all over the world become refugees. A refugee is someone who has fled his or her country, and does not yet have a new homeland. People become refugees for different reasons. For example, you might become a refugee if there was a flood or an earthquake in your area, and you had to leave your native country to stay alive. Sometimes, people become refugees because they belong to a religious or cultural group that those in power want to harm. These people are often forced to leave their homelands because of threats and violence.

when Malalai was a preschooler of four. Many Afghanis fled their country at that time because their lives had become hopeless. People who are either forced out of their homelands, or choose to leave because their lives are too hard or dangerous, are called refugees.

For sixteen years, Malalai and her family lived in refugee camps in Iran and Pakistan, countries bordering Afghanistan. Being in a refugee camp is a strange and difficult experience. You never feel that you have a real home, or that you belong anywhere. You cannot leave, because you don't have any other place to go. Few countries accept refugees as possible citizens, and those that do take a long time to let refugees in. At a refugee camp you live crowded together in tents, and share donated food, water, and necessities with thousands of other people.

Being a refugee also means that you must be ready to leave at a moment's notice. If you've been living in a refugee camp, and a new group of people are expected there, you could be told to pack up everything you can carry and move to another camp. Malalai's family had to move from camp to camp several times just to survive.

In Canada, the United States, and most Western countries, the law insists that both boys and girls must go to school. There were simple tent schools in the camps, but for Malalai and her sisters, it would have been hard to get even a basic education in such a school. For one thing, during wartime, it's sometimes too dangerous to keep the schools open. And there was an even larger difficulty. Even when the schools were open, many girls would not—or could not—attend them. There are powerful leaders in countries such as Iran, Afghanistan, and Pakistan who don't believe that girls need education like boys. In fact, they don't think that girls should even learn to read and write. They believe that a girl's only responsibility is to cook, clean, and take care of her younger brothers and sisters, to learn only what helps her become a wife and mother later on. Because of these powerful opinions, it was mostly boys who attended these camp schools. But Malalai's parents were more modern than most. They made sure that their daughters got the best education that they could, even under terrible living conditions.

In 1998, when Malalai was twenty years old, the Soviet army that had invaded her country finally left Afghanistan for good. Malalai's family decided to go back to the country that they missed so much. They returned home to their beautiful province, but what Malalai found there saddened and upset her. The foreign invaders were gone, but now the ultra-strict Taliban were in power. Malalai soon discovered that for her, living under the Taliban was just as bad—or even worse—than it would have been to live in a country ruled by invaders.

The Taliban who ruled Afghanistan when Malalai and her family returned home are Muslims who believe that their religion must be practiced exactly as it was when the Qur'an was written thousands of years ago. In those times, girls and

SAME RELIGION, DIFFERENT PATHS

Afghanistan is a country where almost all follow the Muslim faith, and live according to the ideas in their holy book, the Qur'an. Muslim people also live in many other countries and make up about a fifth of the world's population. Just like people of any other religion, the 1.5 billion Muslims around the world follow their faith in a variety of different ways. For instance, some Muslim women dress like everyone else, while others wear modest clothing that covers their bodies, and even their heads and faces when they leave their homes. Muslim people do not all follow the same religious customs. They make choices about how they will dress, eat, and pray, depending on what they believe their religion tells them to do.

women did not go to school, or have any goals except to get married and have children.

The Qur'an says that girls and women should cover themselves to be modest. When they go out, the most traditional Muslim women wear long robes, called *hijabs,* which cover them from head to toe, and *burkas,* which cover their faces. Strictly religious women dress this way because, according to ancient Muslim traditions, a woman or girl should only show her face in her home. But many Muslim girls and women all over the world keep their traditions by dressing in clothes that cover them up, yet are modern and easy to move in. Still others dress like everyone else.

The Taliban forced all Afghan women, no matter what their religious feelings, or what they had worn before, to dress in long robes according to ancient religious customs, and to cover their faces before they left their homes. To the Taliban, if a woman shows her body contours or face to a man who isn't in her family, she is a sinner to be harshly punished.

While the Taliban were in power in Afghanistan (they were chased out in 2001), they maintained a kind of religious police. These men patrolled the streets and made sure that women dressed according to their rules. They also decreed that women could

When the Taliban came to power, women were forced to wear burkas so their faces and bodies were hidden when they were in public.

never leave their homes without their husbands, brothers, or fathers, or speak without permission from a male relative or another man. If women broke any of the Taliban's regulations, the police shouted at them, arrested them, beat them, and sometimes even killed them. Often Malalai saw that male passers by just stood and watched these cruelties in fear.

She saw more suffering that upset her. Afghanistan is a very poor country where many people are unemployed. The poor often live without running water or electricity in their homes. Because of the war and invasion, it was very difficult even for farmers to grow food, so many were desperate. And because Afghanistan is a country of high mountain ranges and few roads, those who live in small, isolated villages can't get to doctors or nurses when they become sick.

The girls are taught not to complain if they aren't feeling well, but just to get on with their household chores. Sadly, many Afghan girls who obey that rule do get very sick, and sometimes even die without anyone ever knowing what made them ill.

Malalai understood that she needed to help her people. So, with the help of other caring supporters, she decided to start a secret school that would welcome both boys and girls, something that had never been done in Afghanistan before. She also helped to start health clinics where girls and women had a chance to be examined and treated by doctors and nurses. For the first time in their lives, they could learn important information about their bodies, which all girls and women need to know.

Malalai's actions were extremely brave, because, aside from the Taliban, there are local warlords in Afghanistan who have held absolute power in their villages for thousands of years. They would not want anyone, and certainly not a young, inexperienced woman, to challenge how they had run the country for so long.

Soon, the people in Malalai's area were noticing all the work that she was doing to improve their lives. They persuaded her to represent them in their local government, called the Loya Jirga. Soon she was invited to a special meeting there. At that meeting a warlord who was part of the government said to Malalai, "Even God has not given you equal rights, because under His decision, two women are equal to one man." But Malalai refused to be intimidated. Instead, on her first day as a representative, Malalai gave a short but angry speech attacking the power of the warlords and talking about their crimes in Afghanistan. This single act of a woman who dared to challenge the authority of the men in power drew the attention of the whole world.

From that point on, no one could stop this courageous young woman. In fact, once they had heard about Malalai's powerful speech, her neighbors convinced her to aim even higher. She ran for election to Afghanistan's new parliament and won. At the age of twenty-five, Malalai Joya became Afghanistan's youngest Member of Parliament. At every session of the new government, she spoke out against the power of the warlords or anyone in government who did not want women and girls to have the education and health care that they needed.

But it was not easy for her. At nearly every government meeting, she had her hair pulled, was attacked physically, and was called insulting names by the men. Once, the warlords brought thousands of male protesters to Kabul, the capital city of Afghanistan, to march against her beliefs. The crowd chanted "Death to Joya" through the capital's streets.

During her time in the Afghan government, the attacks on Malalai were constant. The warlords would even distribute negative flyers about her to the public. One of them showed a faked picture of Malalai bareheaded, without her traditional headscarf. The pamphlet declared that she should be banished

Afghan women shout slogans during a demonstration against the parliament's removal of Malalai Joya in Kabul.

from the government because she was immodest and hated her religion. During her two years in parliament she never once had a chance to complete a speech that everyone could hear, because her microphone would be turned off. Still, she fought on.

On May 21, 2007, Malalai's fellow members of parliament voted to suspend her for three years, and so took away her right to speak freely. Since she has been suspended, the Afghan government has prevented Malalai from speaking openly about the problems in her troubled country. Many world leaders and human rights groups have protested to the Afghan government, but to no avail.

Malalai has remained strong and outspoken. She still lives in Afghanistan, and her life is in constant danger. Every day, she receives death threats from people who want to end her protests. In fact, she has been forced to have bodyguards to protect her twenty-four hours a day. But she refuses to be silenced. Since her suspension, Malalai has written a memoir, *Raising My Voice: A Woman Among Warlords,* published in 2009. Her book has been translated into many languages, and is read all over the world. She has traveled internationally, speaking about her life and the problems ordinary Afghanis face. But when she's at home, Malalai is always aware of her enemies. She is so afraid for her life that she moves from one house to another quite frequently. She is always being watched. Whenever she is brave enough to go out in public, she wears a *burka* to cover her features, so that no one can recognize her.

Even though she is very young, Malalai Joya has made an incredible contribution to girls and women in her country. For now, she has been forbidden by the warlords in Afghanistan to speak out against the injustices in her country. But because of her book and her speeches, people who care about human rights are supporting her. The Afghan government is being pressured every day to reinstate her as a member, so that she can continue to speak in public. Malalai and her growing army of supporters worldwide keep in contact by Facebook, Twitter, and e-mail. Malalai Joya's life is a constant struggle, but it is only a matter of time until her pleas for better health care and education for the girls and women of Afghanistan turn into action. Her mission for equality has only just begun.

Sources and Resources

ONÉSIME DORVAL

Famous Canadian Women website. "Famous Canadian Women's Historical Timeline." http://famouscanadian-women.com/timeline/timeline1850-1899.htm

Parks Canada website. "Saskatchewan's First Teacher." http://www.pc.gc.ca/apps/cseh-twih/archives2_E.asp?id=593

The Encyclopedia of Saskatchewan website. "Dorval, Onésime." http://esask.uregina.ca/entry/dorval_one-sime_1845-1932.html

HELEN KELLER AND ANNIE SULLIVAN MACY

Davidson, Margaret. *Helen Keller.* New York: Scholastic Paperbacks, 1989.

Keller, Helen. *The Story of My Life: Parts 1 and 2.* New York: Doubleday and Company, 1905.

Nielsen, Kim E. *Beyond the Miracle Worker: The Remarkable Life of Anne Sullivan Macy and her Extraordinary Friendship with Helen Keller.* Boston: Beacon Press, 2010.

American Foundation for the Blind website. "Anne Sullivan Macy: Miracle Worker." http://www.afb.org/annesullivan/

BookRags website. "Anne Sullivan Macy Biography." http://www.bookrags.com/biography/anne-sullivan-macy-woh/

MARIA MONTESSORI

George, E. Anne and Maria Montessori. *The Montessori Method (Illustrated Edition)*. Charleston, SC: CreateSpace, 2011.

Hainstock, Elizabeth G. *The Essential Montessori: An Introduction to the Woman, the Writings, the Method, and the Movement*. New York: Plume, 1997.

Kramer, Rita. *Maria Montessori: A Biography*. Cambridge, MA: Da Capo Press, 1988.

Montessori, Maria and Paula Polk Lillard. *Montessori: A Modern Approach*. New York: Schocken Books, 1988.

Montessori Australia website. "A Biography of Dr. Maria Montessori." http://montessori.org.au/montessori/biography.htm

Essortment website. "Maria Montessori Biography." http://www.essortment.com/maria-montessori-biography-20482.html

RADEN AYU (OR AYEN) KARTINI

Cote, Joost J., ed. *Realizing the Dream of R. A. Kartini: Her Sister's Letters from Colonial Java*. Athens, OH: Ohio University Press, 2008.

Kartini, Raden Ayen and Agnes Louise Symmers, trans. *Letters of a Javanese Princess*. Whitefish, MT: Kessinger Publishing, 2010.

Ramusack, Barbara N. and Sharon Sievers. *Women in Asia: Restoring Women to History*. Bloomington, IN: Indiana University Press, 1999.

Center for History and New Media website. "Raden Ajeng Kartini." http://chnm.gmu.edu/wwh/modules/lesson12/pdfs/primarysourcepacket.pdf

FRIEDL DICKER-BRANDEIS
Rubin, Susan Goldman. *Fireflies in the Dark: the Story of Friedl Dicker-Brandeis and the Children of Terezin*. New York: Holiday House, 2000.

Volavkova, Hana. *I Never Saw Another Butterfly*. New York: Schocken, 1994.

Wix, Linney. *Through a Narrow Window: Friedl Dicker-Brandeis and her Terezin Students*. Albuquerque, NM: University of New Mexico Press, 2010.

The Jewish Women's Archive website. "Friedl Dicker-Brandeis." http://jwa.org/encyclopedia/article/dicker-brandeis-friedl

Jewish Virtual Library website. "Dicker-Brandeis, Frederike." http://www.jewishvirtuallibrary.org/jsource/judaica/ejud_0002_0005_0_05202.html

MARVA COLLINS
Collins, Marva and Alex Haley. *Marva Collins Way: Updated Edition*. Los Angeles: Tarcher, 1990.

Collins, Marva. *Ordinary Children, Extraordinary Teachers*. Newburyport, MA: Hampton Roads Publishing, 1992.

Collins, P. Kamara Sekou. *The School that Cared: A Story of the Marva Collins Preparatory Academy of Cincinnati.* Lanham, MD: University Press of America, 2003.

Davis, Juanita J., Clara L. Adams Ender, Sharon E. Ferguson-Roberts, Rita G. Giles, and Johnnie H. Miles. *Almanac of African American Heritage: Chronicle.*

"Marva Collins Built Success on 'Tough' Teaching." *The Chicago Sun-Times.* March 1, 1990.

Marva Collins website. "Marva N. Collins Biography." http://www.marvacollins.com/biography.html

CHRISTA MCAULIFFE

Burgess, Colin. *Teacher in Space: Christa McAuliffe and the Challenger Legacy.* Lincoln, NE: University of Nebraska Press, 2000.

Corrigan, Grace George. *A Journal for Christa: Christa McAuliffe, Teacher in Space.* Lincoln, NE: University of Nebraska Press, 2000.

Jeffrey, Laura S. *Christa McAuliffe: A Space Biography (Countdown to Space).* Berkeley Heights, NJ: Enslow Publishers, 1998.

E-Skolar website. "Christa McAuliffe Biography." http://e-skolar.com/docs/christa-mcauliffe-biography.html

The Challenger Center website. "S. Christa McAuliffe: Payload Specialist Astronaut and Teacher in Space." http://www.challenger.org/about/history/mcauliffe.cfm

"Now Grown Up, the Students who Loved Christa McAuliffe Pass Her Legacy to New Generation." Winnipeg Free Press. January 23, 2011. Available at http://www.winnipegfreepress.com/world/breakingnews/now-grown-up-the-students-who-loved-christa-mcauliffe-pass-her-legacy-to-new-generation-114459574.html

DENISE FRUCHTER
Blostein, David A. and Denise Fruchter. *Other People.* Muskoka, ON: Camp Winston and The Pine Bay Foundation, 2011.

"Where Kids Get What They Need." *The Globe and Mail.* June 4, 2007. Available at http://www.theglobeandmail.com/life/where-kids-get-what-they-need/article793072/page2/

"Camp Winston Welcomed Errant Camper." *The Toronto Star.* July 14, 2010. Available at http://www.thestar.com/freshairfund/article/835826--camp-winston-welcomed-errant-camper

"At Camp Winston, Kids 'Tic Together.'" July 12, 2007. http://www.thestar.com/FreshAirFund/article/235108

ERIN GRUWELL
Gruwell, Erin, The Freedom Writers, and Zlata Filipovic. *The Freedom Writers Diary: How a Teacher and 150 Teens Used Writing to Change Themselves and the World Around Them.* New York: Broadway Books, 2009.

Gruwell, Erin. *Teach from Your Heart: Lessons I Learned from the Freedom Writers.* New York: Broadway Books, 2008.

Gruwell, Erin, The Freedom Writers, and Anna Quindlen. *Teaching Hope: Stories from the Freedom Writer Teachers and Erin Gruwell.* New York: Broadway Books, 2009.

Freedom Writers Foundation website. "About Erin Gruwell." http://www.freedomwritersfoundation.org/site/c. kqIXL2PFJtH/b.2259999/apps/s/content.asp?ct=3290463

The Healthy Times website. "Freedom Writers: An Exclusive Interview with Erin Gruwell." http://www.healthytimesonline.com/archives/freedom_ writers.htm

MALALAI JOYA

Heath, Jennifer and Ashraf Zahedi. *Land of the Unconquerable: The Lives of Contemporary Afghan Women.* Berkeley: University of California Press, 2011.

Joya, Malalai and O'Keefe, Derrick. *A Woman among Warlords: the Extraordinary Story of an Afghan who Dared to Raise Her Voice.* New York: Simon and Shuster, 2009.

Afghan Women's Mission website. "A Woman among Warlords." http://www.afghanwomensmission.org/?p=169

"Liberation Was Just a Big Lie." *The Toronto Star.* November 19, 2009. Available at http://www. thestar.com/news/canada/afghanmission/ article/727873---liberation-was-just-a-big-lie

Acknowledgments

Writing this book has been an amazing learning experience for me. I would like to express my appreciation to Margie Wolfe and the staff of Second Story Press—Emma Rodgers and Phuong Truong for their assistance. My particular thanks go to Carolyn Jackson and Melissa Kaita for their efforts in the editing and production of this book.

I would also like to offer my heartfelt gratitude to my editor Sheba Meland whose kindness, guidance, and love of language so enhanced my own work.

Photo Credits

COVER PHOTOS
(L-R): courtesy NASA, New York World-Telegram and the Sun Newspaper Photograph Collection (Library of Congress) LC-USZ62-1215, courtesy The Freedom Writers Foundation, © Bettmann/CORBIS, AfghanKabul/Creative Commons

ONÉSIME DORVAL
page 5: Saskatchewan Archives Board RA-12843

HELEN KELLER AND ANNIE SULLIVAN MACY
page 13: Library of Congress LC-USZ62-78983
page 18: courtesy Jeri Alice Cripps
page 20: Library of Congress LC-USZ62-112513
page 21: Library of Congress LC-USZ62-13123
page 25: Library of Congress LC-USZ62-111737

MARIA MONTESSORI
page 27: New York World-Telegram and the Sun Newspaper Photograph Collection (Library of Congress) LC-USZ62-121591
page 34: Library of Congress LC-DIG-hec-03471

RADEN AYU KARTINI
page 37: Tropenmuseum of the Royal Tropical Institute (KIT)

FRIEDL DICKER-BRANDEIS

page 54: From *Hana's Suitcase*, by Karen Levine, Second Story Press, 2002, courtesy of George Brady and Family, and the Terezin Ghetto Museum

MARVA COLLINS

page 59: © Bettmann/CORBIS
page 65: © Bettmann/CORBIS
page 68: © Bettmann/CORBIS

CHRISTA MCAULIFFE

All photos courtesy NASA

DENISE FRUCHTER

page 81: courtesy Camp Winston

ERIN GRUWELL

page 91: courtesy The Freedom Writers Foundation

MALALAI JOYA

page 99: AfghanKabul/Creative Commons
page 103: Creative Commons
page 106: © AHMAD MASOOD/Reuters/Corbis

More from the Women's Hall of Fame Series

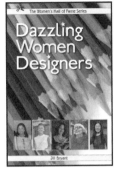

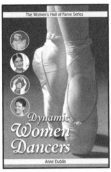

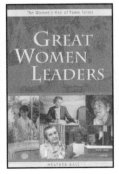
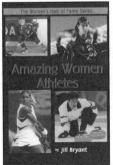

ages 9-13 • $10.95 • www.secondstorypress.ca